Live Longer

Professor Hilton Hotema

ISBN: 978-1-63923-122-5

Printed: February 2022
Cover Art By: Paul Amid

Published and Distributed By:
Lushena Books
607 Country Club Drive, Unit E
Bensenville, IL 60106
www.lushenabks.com

ISBN: 978-1-63923-122-5

Live Longer

Table of Contents

Notice To All Concerned

Be it known all men by these presents that statements contained in this volume are based on facts observed and facts inferred, the known laws of Creation, the statements of the Bible, and other ancient scriptures as they are and have beeen interpreted.

No claim is made intentionally as to what any method cited may do for any one in any case, and it is recognized and understood that the author and publisher of this work assume no responsibility for any opinion presented or expressed, nor the results that may occur in any case wherein any one may decide to pursue any path mentioned in this work.

The author of this work is not available for engagements, receives no visitors, grants no interviews, and has no desire to become Exhibit A for curiosity seekers. He has no message for the public except those contained in his writings, and he discusses with no one the matters about which he writes.

The publisher of this work has no authority to give any one the address of the author, nor to comment upon the opinions expressed or the postulates presented in these writings. His engagement is to publish and sell the work, and there his obligation ends.

Professor Hilton Hotema
Honolulu, 1967

<u>Chapter No. 1</u>
Right Living

"The groups and nations in which industrial civilization has attained its highest development are precisely those that are becoming weaker. But they do not realize it. They are without protection against the hostile surroundings that science has built about them. In truth, our civilization has created certain conditions of existence which render life itself impossible," (Doctor Alexis Carrel, in *Man The Unknown* page 28).

Living organisms have no existence independent of the Life Principle. They are an expression of the Principle and not productive of it.

The duration of a living body is, barring accidents, determined by a definite law of the Universe, and the body sinks into degeneracy and comes to an end when its composition ceases to harmonize with that law or when the Environment is hostile to its existence. The coming of the end may be sudden or delayed, depending on the degrees of the shock sustained by the body from the hostile elements or the Environment.

For instance, man may live 50 or 100 years under certain conditions discordant to his being, or he may die suddenly as where he enters a chamber of poisonous gas.

Two definite factors appear to determine man's duration. These are (1) Environment and (2) habits.

Habits are man's mode of living. They may be good or bad and are subject to his will.

Environment constitutes man's surroundings as his home, place of employment, the region in which he lives. Whether good or bad, he cannot change the condition of his Environment so easily as he can his habits.

Carrel says, "We are constantly being made by our Environment and by our self" (our habits). — Ibid.

The power of Environment is so strong in the case of man that Doctor Robert Walter wrote: "Every fact of life goes to prove that man is made what he is by the molding influence of his environments." (*Vital Science,* page 252).

The world's leading authors appear almost to ignore the fact that a power so potent that it constantly molds man's existence and shapes his destiny, had great influence in the process that brought man first into physical being.

In his book *Pre-Adamites* (1899), Doctor Alexander Winchell wrote, "Man made his advent in a region where the elements did not oppose his coming." (page 336).

Winchell's statement is directly to the point but to limited. Man could not appear as a physical being until the elements, which continue to mold his body, were so perfect for his birth that he was drawn out of potential existence into actual physical being as a potential chick is drawn from the egg and becomes an actual chick, But the egg must be placed in the proper environment, otherwise the physical chick cannot come into being.

Everything is, something never comes from nothing, and what appears actually must exist potentially. The potential becomes the actual only when proper conditions prevail. The egg and chick are good examples that demonstrate this law.

Everything is subject to that cosmic law. Man is no exception. He owes his physical being to the work of that law, and he sinks into degeneracy and death when he violates that law.

"Perfect correspondence would be perfect life. Were there no changes in the environment but such as the organism had adapted changes to meet, and were it never to fail in the efficiency with which it met them, there would be eternal existence and eternal knowledge," (First Principles.)

Spencer explains the law that makes eternal life in the flesh possible. Simply supply the requisite conditions. Of his observations Drummond said:

"He is analyzing with minute care the relation between Environment and Life (Living organism). He unfolds the principle according to which Life is high or low, long or short. He shows why organisms live and why they die; and finally he defines a condition of things in which an organism would never die — in which it would enjoy a perpetual and perfect life."

Drummond then shows that man, by reason of his more complex organism is better equipped with adapted changes than is any other animal to meet and master, or control, we had better say, his Environment. He wrote:

"The organism then with the most perfect set or correspondence, that is, the highest and most complex organism, has an obvious advantage over less complex forms. It can adjust itself more perfectly and frequently. But this is just the biological way of saying that it can live the longest. Hence, the relation between complexity may be expressed thus — the most complex organisms are the longest lived."

Drummond agrees with all facts and findings which indicate that man is made to live longer than other creatures on earth. Yet he does well to live seventy years. If he lives a century, it is considered remarkable.

The poor showing man makes in this respect is proven by a comparison of his lifespan with that of the birds and beasts.

According to naturalists, the rook, crow, and pelican life span is 100 years and more. The swan lives 300 years. Tacitus said the eagle lives 500 years. Some of the parrot species are said to live in their native environment for 500 and 600 years. The despicable swine, in its native environment, lives to the great age of 300 years. Whales are said to live 1,000 years, and alligators, 1500 years.

It seems neither reasonable nor probable that man, nature's masterpiece, the most perfect of all living creatures, should have a shorter lifespan than the fowls of the air and the beasts of the field over which he was given dominion *(Genesis 1:28)*.

It is well to remember that these animals have not done what man has. They have remained in the Environment with which their organisms harmonize and correspond, while he has not.

The Law of Environment, or of Correspondence as Spencer called it, cannot be violated with impunity.

If all the earth were a polar region, perpetually covered with ice and snow, the Germ of Life would still exist, but it could not, under such hostile conditions, manifest its presence in physical form.

In such a hostile region, Living Creatures could not come into physical being. In such a region they were never produced. The fact that some now live in such a place is merely evidence of their hardiness. It adds nothing to their lifespan, but takes much away.

The results of every investigation point to the tropics as the Natural Home of Man. Professor Winchell wrote:

"Man, as an animal, is unclothed and possessed of a delicate skin. All naked land-animals are natives of warm countries; and they must be to induce the ordinary climatic

4

vicissitudes. Man, similarly made his advent on earth in a region where the elements did not oppose his coming. Primitively, he is a tropical animal and wandered into the colder zones only as he learned to protect himself with artificial coverings" (*Pre-Adamites,* page 356).

That law governing man's physical origin has not changed. Neither has his constitution. That law shows that —

1. Correspondence must obtain and prevail as between the Living Organism and its Environment. That is the condition of physical existence. Man could not come into physical being until the favorable conditions of his Environment prepared the way.

2. The health standard of the organism can be no better than that of the Environment.

Bananas do not grow in a cold climate because their constitution does not harmonize with such climate. Salt water fish do not live in fresh water because their constitution does not harmonize with fresh water.

Man is superior to both bananas and fish by reason of his great power of adaptability. He is able to survive for a few miserable years under the strain of habits and Environment so destructive that they would otherwise cause sudden death and in fact do sometimes.

The Law of Correspondence in this case means that a harmonious condition must exist between living things and their Environment, or they will die and disappear. That does occur occasionally, causing certain vegetation and animals to become extinct.

When Spencer formulated the Law of Eternal Physical Life, he sought to show that Death is the final result of changes in the Environment which the Living Organism had not adapted changes to meet, thus causing a condition of discord that ends in physical death. And he is right.

Medical art makes no investigation of this line of thought because it has discovered no satisfactory way to explain the Law of Animation. It holds that the body functions because it functions and that decrepitude and death are the direct result of wear and tear on the organism.

Advanced physiologists have discovered that vital function is so perfect, and the body is so perfectly constituted, that it possesses the power to prolong its existence by adapting itself to adverse conditions that would otherwise cause not only early death, but instant death in many cases.

On this point Doctor Charles W. Greene wrote:

"As the air expired from the lungs contains a large proportion of carbon dioxide and a small amount of organic matter, it is obvious if the same air is breathed again and again, the proportion of these elements will constantly increase until the air becomes unfit to breathe.

"It is a remarkable fact that the organism, after a time, adapts to a very vitiated atmosphere and that a person soon comes to breathe without sensible inconvenience an atmosphere which, when he first enters it, feels intolerable. But such an adaptation can occur only at the expense of a depression of all the vital functions, which must be injurious if long continued or often respected." (*Physiology,* page 286)

In those few words, Greene tells a great story. It would require a large book to tell what occurs in the case of those who live and labor in air so foul that the body must "get used to it" before the person can tolerate it.

That "getting used to it" includes many things. It means depressed vital functions says Greene. It means symptoms of languor, fatigue, a sense of oppression, headache, backache, rheumatism, enervation, toxemia, palpitation of the heart, apnea, dyspnea, dysphoria, hyperpnea, hyperpyremia, diptheria, mumps, measles, whooping cough, scarlet-fever, chickenpox, smallpox, influenza, pneumonia, etc.

The victims suffering from these symptoms of degeneration are taught to look for relief in foods, tonics, stimulants, vaccines, serum drugs. No one tells them of the dangers of polluted air and a hostile environment.

Human ailments in the United States have built up a five-billion-dollar-a-year business; and it increases as the population increases. The powers that be permit nothing to be done to damage or decrease this profitable business.

Chapter No. 2
Healthful Environment

"Man lives a natural life in the tropics and supports himself with fruits of the palm tree. He is only existing in other parts of the world and lives miserably on grains, tubers, and meats." — *Linnacus, the Great Naturalist.*

In 1944 an article appeared in Health Culture magazine under *"A Nation Without Cancer,"* by "Medicus" in which were published various excerpts from the works of a Doctor Tipper, said to be "a distinguished London Surgeon," who "spent twenty years in Southern Nigeria in the pay of the British Government's West African Medical Service."

The story means so much to the suffering souls in the Zone of Hibernation who are hunting for health that it should be blazoned across the sky in letters of fire.

Nigeria is a small tropical region situated just north of the Equator, blessed with that friendly climate which prevailed in the biblical Garden of Eden, where the people were naked and not uncomfortable *(Genesis 2).*

During his long stay in Nigeria, Tipper "exercised his acute observation in studying the physique, health, habits and customs of the great Palm Belt that stretches miles inland," says the account.

What did Tipper say of the physical, mental, and economic condition of those natives? He reported them to be — "Amazingly vigorous, full of laughter, reveling in physical and social activity, while possessing no architecture, no literature, and no mechanical inventions and shut off from civilization by the Sahara (desert) for thousands of years."

In other words, these fortunate people are (1) free of the tainted touch of that artificialism miscalled civilization and, consequently, they are (2) free of the effects, the distress, poverty, and misery that results from living that artificial life termed civilization.

These people appear to be living close to the Fundamental Plan *(Genesis 2:7, 8, 9, 25),* and, accordingly, they are enjoying the health, happiness, and economic freedom that result from living as they do.

If there is any other means of escape from the effects, distress, poverty, misery, and suffering that results from living that artificial life erroneously called civilization, no one has ever found it.

Here appears the solution of human problems. Here lies the cause of human distress, and here appears the remedy. So simple as to be understood by a child, yet so profound that a commercialized science cannot comprehend it.

Be it known that modern science is not actuated by a desire to improve that state of man. So said that great scientist, Alexis Carrel in his book, *Man, The Unknown.* In describing the artificial state called civilized, he said:

"It has been erected without any knowledge of our great nature. It was born from the whims of scientific discoveries from the appetites of men, their illusions, their theories, and their desires. Although constructed by our efforts, it is not adjusted to our size and shape.

"Obviously, science follows no plan. It develops at random. Its progress depends on fortuitous conditions, such as the birth of men of genius, the form of their minds, the direction taken by their curiosity. It is not at all actuated by a desire to improve the state of human beings.

9

"The discoveries responsible for industrial civilization were brought forth by the fancy of the scientists' institutions and of the more or less casual circumstances of their careers — Men of science do not know where they are going. They are guided by chance." (page 23).

Are you willing to trust your fate to and follow a group of men who know not where they are going and are guided only by accident and chance?

A world of scientists without any science. No one can make anything else out of Carrel's statements. They have no goal; they know not where they are going; they are guided only by accident and chance. And they are the builders of what we have and are called scientists.

Get down on your knees, ye misled multitude, and worship the blind fools whom ye follow. Examine your mental, physical, and economic condition and behold the result of worshiping the blind fools whom ye follow. As they know not where they are going, neither do you. As they are guided only by accident and chance, so are you.

The ignorant, uncultured, uncivilized heathens of tropical Nigeria, as scientists would term them, are not following these scientists. They are following the Fundamental Plan of Human Life. They are guided by a Natural Science known not to civilization, and they possess, according to Tipper —

Certain fundamental sanities that challenge the much-vaunted superiority of the white man of civilization. These sanities mean no cancer, no appendicitis, no syphilis, none of the white man's diseases. Their teeth are beautiful, their digestion clean, their vitality tremendous, their spirits high. And they are great farmers.

Compare this glorious picture with the condition of the millions in civilization. And the rulers of our nation are spending billions of dollars of the taxpayers' money in their search of what these natives have and come before you with empty hands.

Eureka! Here it is. The long search is ended. The goal has been found. A science that is science. The natural Science, unknown to the scientists of civilization.

All we need to do is to turn back to Natural Science, to the Fundamental Plan, and the things we most desire will be given unto us. According to Tipper –

"The Bene negro not only knows how to grow his own food to perfection, but the women know how to prepare and blend it to perfection.

"There are no sugar refineries, no flour mills, no bread, beef, mutton, or pork. He grows a variety of fruits, vegetables, and nuts. His bread is the yam, a pumpkin-like tuber that he pounds into a pulp. For sugar he has the pure sugarcane; he has no lollies to leech the calcium from his teeth and tissues, for fruits he has bananas, oranges, pears, papayas, pine apples, and limes.

"It is worth noting that their long experience and traditions have led them to place a supreme value on vegetables."

With no tax-eating department of agriculture, county agents, and "food experts," the Bene people know how to grow their food to perfection. It has always been thus with the tribes in the tropics who live naturally and in harmony with the Fundamental Law.

Man never forgot how to grow his own food to perfection while he lived on the land. But he lost the art when he left the land and went to labor in the artificial sweat-shops of a heartless industrialism, where he voluntarily, in his ignorance, made himself the helpless slave of those who rule him.

Ages of that sort of living have made the man of civilization so helpless and dependent, that he knows almost nothing now about growing his own food on the land.

No bread, no beef, no mutton, no pork. What does the healthy Bene negro eat to be "amazingly vigorous" and to possess vitality tremendous?

Many times the people of the socialized pattern of civilization have demanded tests to prove whether a strict vegetarian diet is better than the common diet of civilization.

Here is that test and here are the results. When we hear the meat trust say that meat is necessary for health and vigor, we will know the statement is false.

"Their teeth are beautiful." Examine the teeth of this rotten civilization. just as rotten as the civilization in which we live.

The diet that builds the body also builds the teeth. If that diet is bad and builds a deficient body, it also builds defective teeth.

Now a lesson for the misled mothers of civilization. According to Tipper—

"The Bene mother will suckle her baby for two years, then wean her child on vegetable broth, which she prepares from vegetables and herbs. Later the child is fed more solid vegetables and fruit, but no bread. There is no bread in Nigeria."

"Tipper says that the Bene negro on his small or large farm wears very loose, light clothing, nothing on his head to exclude the ultraviolet sun rays. He eats twice a day and moves his bowels twice a day. The feces are soft, and constipation and piles are unknown troubles. Physically, vitally, and emotionally, he is a free and splendid specimen of the genus Homo."

It may be, think we, that the Bene negro is naturally more hardy and vigorous than the white man of civilization. The matter should be tested by having one of them live as civilized man lives. The result would furnish reliable evidence to prove the point in question.

A splendid suggestion. That was done. What was the result? Just what an intelligent person would expect. According to Tipper –

"A village chief's son was sent to a coast town to be educated, passing thence to some petty commercial job, aping white man's habits in clothes, food, and all the rest — and rapidly degenerated both physically and mentally. Appendicitis, gastritis, stomach ulcer, and cancer appeared in due course."

There is the test case, and there is the result. There is the cause, and there is the effect. But without removing the cause, medical art searches far and wide for remedies to cure the effect.

If we live in the Zone of Hibernation as civilized man does, we will have all his aches and pains, disorders and degeneracy. If we live in the Zone of Eternal Life, as the natives live in their garden of perpetual spring, we will have all their vitality and their economic freedom,

This is too simple and too understandable for the misled multitude in the Zone of Hibernation. Only a few wise ones here and there in every generation will see the light and migrate to some tropical region, back to the Natural Home of Humanity, and there find health, happiness, and economic freedom.

Be assured that the Fundamental Plan plays no favorites and has no "chosen people" *(Deuteronomy 7:6)*. Those who choose to live according to the Fundamental Plan will receive the blessings of life.

Chapter No. 3
Climate

As yet we (doctors) do not know what environment is the most favorable for the optimum development of civilized man. The environment that molded the body and soul of our ancestors during many millenniums has now been replaced by another. This silent revolution has occurred gradually and almost without our noticing it. We have not realized its importance. But it is one of the most dramatic events in human history. For any modification in their surroundings inevitably and profoundly disturbs all living beings. For we are constantly being made by our environment and by our self. (Carrel in *Man, The Unknown*).

In those words, volumes are said that bear directly on human health and longevity. They make almost no impression on the misled multitude. It's too simple, clear, and understandable. Yet those words describe the chief cause of man's ailments and early death.

Health, longevity, and friendly climate go together. Man's physical existence is governed by and depends upon climate. Also his health and the length of his life-span.

In the hunt for the highway to health, we are forever meeting that condition which Spencer said must prevail between body and environment in order not only to preserve health and promote longevity, but to produce that Physical Immortality which Carrel's experiments demonstrated is possible.

Man is the highest and noblest of living creatures, the only being on earth capable of reason and judgment and endowed with powers of intelligence for carrying into execution such arts and designs as science may invent and and philosophy may discover.

That exalted being comes not so near, by far to fulfilling his purpose on earth, with respect to health and longevity, as the ape or baboon.

The fishes of the sea, the fowls of the air, and the beasts of the field fit perfectly into their environment. Even the spider and the snake, except for the interference of man, are perfectly adapted to their environment. But civilized man appears as a renegade and an outcast.

Created to have dominion "over every living thing upon the earth" *(Genesis1:20),* man is a slave of the economic problem, a prisoner of the hostile environment that he himself has built, and a victim of the evil habits he has formed.

From Master of the Visible World, man has become the child of superstition, stupidity, selfishness, lustfulness. He regards life as a frolic and permits pleasure, fear, superstition and selfishness to supply the incentive for his every action. And his existence in the world is that of a transgressor. It is divorced from all law and order and ruled by accident and chance.

Instead of learning and obeying the Law of Life and being a part of nature, as are the lower animals, he violates the law and lives apart from Nature. His maxim is. "any way but the natural way."

Natural science shows that living existence depends upon (1) Environment and (2) Adaptation.

(1) Environment. — Man could come into physical being only in an environment where climate and production were perfectly adapted to the full requirements of his organism.

The living organism cannot be modified to make it harmonize with a hostile environment without decreasing its vitality and damaging its integrity. As where a man decreases . his vitality by poisoning his body with nicotine until he can smoke without discomfort he felt when he first attempted to smoke his more vital body fought against the poison.

By permitting the nicotine to damage his nerves and decrease his vitality, smoking becomes possible with some degree of comfort, even though the poison is stealthily destroying the body by slow degrees.

In a similar manner, a hostile environment damages the nerves and decreases the body's vitality until it will tolerate surroundings that surreptitiously destroy it by inches.

While the body is slowly degenerating and dying by degrees, the victim experiences much suffering thru the years as a rule, and the symptoms of that suffering are termed diseases by the doctors and treated as enemies that are trying to throttle the life out of the body.

Carrel says, "Man is a stranger in the (artificial) world he created. He is without protection against the hostile surroundings which civilization has built about him." *(Man, The Unknown)*.

(2) Adaptation. — Making suitable or fit; fitness; the modification of an organism in response to its environment; harmonious relationship between a living body and its environment. — Dictionary.

a. The Frigid Arctic Zone is an environment of perpetual ice and snow. There scarcity rules and poverty reigns. In that hostile environment, man soon perishes.

b. The Tropic Zone is an environment of perpetual fruits and flowers. In that hospitable climate, plenty rules and prosperity reigns. In that environment, man came into physical being; and there he should have perfect health and a life-span of a thousand years.

No factor beyond man's control affects his body so much as climate. Climate conditions the environment. A cold climate makes a hostile environment that builds a sickly body, while a warm climate makes a hospitable environment that builds a healthy body. Only slight reference to the subject of climate is necessary to show an intelligent person in what region of the earth he is made to live.

The climate of the earth has been divided into three principle zones: Frigid, Temperate, and Tropical.

1. The Frigid is the Zone of Eternal Death. Its intense cold and perpetual snow and ice make living there impossible.

2. The Temperate is the Zone of Partial Death. It is the Zone of Winter Sleep, Hibernation, a state of semi-death in which the vital functions of animals and plants fall to the lowest point possible without death ensuing.

Vegetables and animals natural to that zone are peculiarly constituted by Nature so that they have the ability to sink into deep sleep in Winter. The animals not so constituted are clad in heavy coats of warm fur.

When man first migrated to the Temperate Zone, he was forced to clothe his body with the hides of these fur-clad animals that he murdered, in violation of the law of God. That was the birth of the clothing industry. It rose from the transgression of God's laws and has evolved into an economic burden that does its part to crush man in the cold zone.

In the Zone of Hibernation, man pays billions of dollars annually to clothing and fuel mongers for clothes and fuel to protect him from the killing cold. This huge economic burden is unknown to the natives of the tropics, and brought it upon himself by living where he is not made to live.

The climate of the so-called Temperate Zone is the most treacherous on earth. It appears as a snare, set to catch the uninformed. Baited with a season of agreeable weather to entice people into its folds, it then blights their lives forever and sends them to premature graves with its blistering summer heat and its bitter winter blizzards.

Directly and indirectly, it has killed millions in this Nation in the past century. It fills the region where it reigns with sickness, suffering, misery, poverty, despair, early death. It forces people to sell their lives in Economic Slavery to provide artificial clothing, artificial shelter, and artificial heat, not needed in the tropics, but so necessary in the Zone of Hibernation to protect people from the killing cold, that is has developed the worst system of profit, graft, and greed in human history.

3. The Tropics is the Zone of Eternal Life. It is the Zone of Perpetual Summer and supplies food incessantly, spontaneously produced by nature.

Commercialism and industrialism dislike the Tropic Zone because Nature's plentiful production there furnishes man's natural needs and frees him from wage slavery without which these organized institutions that flourish on man's ignorance and economic needs would perish.

That must be the main reason why reports and text-books depict the Tropics as a region suitable only for beasts, reptiles, and the natives who live there.

The Effect of Environment on man is great and powerful. It governs his habits and mode of living. He must adjust himself, his habits, and mode of living to meet the conditions of his Environment.

Clothing, shelter, and fuel are a highly essential part of a cold Environment. Man must have these to protect himself from the killing weather of a cold region.

Man is bound by his Environment — as with bands of steel. He cannot free himself from its influence, nor escape the consequences of its work. In a word, man is what his Environment makes him; and climate makes Environment.

Good health and bad health are conditions that rise from the reactions of man's body to his Environment and his habits. The only remedy for bad health is to remove the cause, and not the treatment of the symptoms.

That puts the matter on a positive, definite, and scientific basis. It removes all the mystery, speculation, and confusion in which medical art had bad health involved.

1. Good health is the lawful product of good climate, good environment, and good habits.

2. Bad health is the lawful product of bad climate, bad environment, and bad habits.

All so simple that it exposes and explodes the sweetest racket on earth and shows how foolish it is for supposedly intelligent persons to write a library of technical books to explain a problem that a child can understand.

Creation constantly requires the presence of certain climatic and environmental conditions for the operation of its processes. These processes cannot produce a coconut grove in the Arctic Zone, a school of fish on dry land, nor a forest in a desert.

A matter that simple must be concealed in technical volumes in order to keep the masses from learning the facts. The job has been so well done those authors of the books are as badly confused as the man in the street.

Living organisms and plants cannot come into actual being until all conditions are such as to bring them into actual being.

The egg contains a potential chick, but the chick will never become reality unless the egg is surrounded by certain definite conditions. One of these is an atmospheric temperature constantly close to 103 degrees Fahrenheit for a certain length of time. Slight variations of the heat either up or down are fatal to the potential chick in the egg.

This law is not nullified by the birth of the chick. After the chick is created and becomes a physical reality, it will still perish if not surrounded by certain conditions. If the variation from these conditions is so slight as not to cause death immediately, or within a few hours or a few days, then death comes on by imperceptible degrees, by a process of degeneration creeping over the creature so gradually and slowly that the fact is not known until the end is near.

Then the fact is misunderstood and misinterpreted by an ignorant world, by people in darkness, and death is attributed to various and imaginary causes gradually termed diseases by medical art, whose members disclose their own ignorance by the fact that many of them die when they should be in their prime.

Man's presence on earth is primarily and directly the result of climatic conditions that made possible his physical appearance: They had to be ideal and perfect, as the egg and the chick. They had to be favorable and not opposed to his coming. Otherwise he could not have come into a visible being from the Spiritual World.

Climatic conditions had to be tropical and free from freezing weather. They had to be capable of producing spontaneously all things needed and necessary for man's welfare and comfort, or he would have perished,

For man was then a child, unable to produce anything and wholly dependent upon the Power, Climate, and Environment that brought him forth from potential existence into the physical world. He could not provide for himself, for he was a helpless infant in the lap of Mother Nature. To her he looked for everything; and if she ever failed him, he perished.

That law of Creation is still in force. Nor has it changed. Man is as fully subject to its provisions now as when he first became a physical being. That Law will never fail him whenever he trusts himself to its provisions and power. When he violates that law, he cannot escape the penalty.

The misled multitude, bound by the social pattern, kept in darkness, stumbling thru the ages, worshiping every object from a wooden image to a golden calf, never understood, and does not understand now, that the Law of Creation has definite and positive requirements.

Modern science is unable to shake off the ignorance of the dark ages, to free itself from the thralls of its absurd theory of Evolution and apply intelligence to the subject of human existence.

Were all the earth a polar region, perpetually covered with ice and snow, potential man would still exist; but he could never manifest on the physical plane.

In that hostile region, living organisms were not produced on the physical plane. The fact that some now live in such reasons is just more evidence of their hardiness. It takes much from their life while adding nothing to it.

No geologist ever searches for the Garden of Eden as being a land of ice and snow. No doctor worthy of the title ever tells his patients to go to the Arctic Zone for health. No scientist will say that frigid weather is favorable for living creatures.

Chapter No. 4
Man's Home

"There is a scientific reason why no part of the Adamite period is more strongly emphasized by the sacred scribe than the perpetually warm climate of the Edenic World. Man dwelling naked in his Eden climate says in language clear and plain that there was in the Fundamental Plan of Life no alternative of summer or winter. This eternal summer climate is necessary to make complete the harmony of the ancient historian's account." — Professor I. N. Vail.

The Fundamental Plan of Human Life is plain and explicit. Man by nature and constitution is a tropical being, made to live in a tropical region.

Health is the normal state of the living organism, which is subject to Law. That Law teaches that: —

Natural living is the highway to health.

Natural living is impossible in a hostile climate.

Therefore, health is impossible in a hostile climate.

Man craves health and longevity, but he lives under conditions that kill him by degrees and often very suddenly.

Summer heat waves in the Temperate Zone kill thousands over the nation. Winter blizzards in the same region kill other thousands. Year after year toxic fumes, gases, smoke, soot, and acids, polluting the air of the nation, kill still more thousands.

Science tries to soften the tone of the picture by asserting that these things kill only the weaker ones, leaving the stronger to improve the race. An intelligent person knows that conditions so bad that they kill the weaker also weaken the stronger and kill them in time.

Biologists show that: —

1. In the region where physical man first appeared and was appointed and constituted to live, ample provisions for his health and economic needs were made by his Maker. Out of that natural location the four major economic problems are clothing, shelter, food, and fuel.

2. To produce these necessities in a hostile environment, man spends his best days in weakening toil, under degenerative conditions, and these deteriorate his organism and send him to an early grave, while suffering many maladies before somatic death ends his miseries.

3. By returning to his Natural Home, man is able, at one stroke, to sweep away the health destroying conditions and economic problems of the day and to secure a state of health that would add years to his life and life to his years.

Man in the cold zone is crushed by his economic burden. It is a law, not noticed by economic experts nor recognized by the masses, that the economic problem grows greater as the productive season grows shorter, while it grows less as the productive season grows longer.

Economic freedom is gained by living on the land in a productive region that is free from the destructive agencies of sizzling summers, blighting droughts, and blasting blizzards. These hostile elements increase the economic problem. They destroy our health, the fruits of our toil, and reduce us to poverty.

Then science takes up the effect of a hostile climate and says that poverty is the cause of many ailments.

Daily toilers are economic slaves. Their enslavement increases in ratio with the decrease in production. That law explains why those in cold climates must toil all the time. Where frost and freeze come not, where droughts do not destroy, there Nature produces abundantly, and little human labor is needed. In our southern states, the natives work less than those in colder regions; and in the tropics, the natives do very little work.

This law shows us how to solve the economic worries that put wrinkles in our face and decrepitude in our body. When we solve the economic problem, we remove our greatest burden. This problem is reduced to the very minimum in the tropics.

Man cannot isolate himself from the circumstances of his surroundings. He is controlled by his Environment, above which he cannot rise to any appreciable extent. But he has the power to leave a hostile environment and migrate to a better one.

That is silently being done on a much larger scale than the masses in the cold zone realize. From 1940 to 1950 the population of California and Florida increased far more than that of any other state of the Union. People are leaving the cold zone and going also to Cuba, Mexico, and Central America.

So far as physical and spiritual qualities are concerned, man is the most regular of all creatures. He could come into physical being only in a land with a regular climate of eternal summer. In such climate only can he maintain himself at his spiritual, physical, and economic best.

The vertical rays of the tropical sun produce the richest developments of the vegetable kingdom. No human labor is needed. These products, as food, are man's only natural food, and they build the best bodies.

As man departs from what even climate and productive land, traveling away from the tropical belt that circles the globe, a gradual decline in the production and development of vegetation occurs, with an increase in the economic problem, until finally the barren regions of the frigid zone are reached, where all development and production end and the economic problem attains its zenith.

Economic slaves have little time in which to acquire much knowledge. They are not noted for wisdom. The position they occupy is proof of their mental inferiority. They are the servants of their more ambitious and better educated masters. They spend their days in weakening toil, with no opportunity for mental and spiritual development. They look for enlightenment and leadership to those who live on the fruits of their labor. These are principally the preacher, doctor, lawyer, and capitalist. Proper knowledge frees man from these snares.

The great races of ancient days developed in tropical and semi-tropical regions. Man's migration into colder zones is a comparatively recent event. It was necessary for genius first to invent many things to provide artificial means of comfort in the hostile climate of the cold zone.

The hostile climate of the cold zone forces man to toil to provide for his needs. He asks his more energetic brother for work that he may live. His brother is not his keeper and is under no obligations to hire him. It is his Maker, not his brother, who is responsible for his being and owes him a living. In the warm regions of the earth that living is abundantly provided.

No human system of economics can correct the evils rising naturally from artificial conditions. These conditions are the product of a hostile climate and the result of man's inventions as he struggles against the law of his being to live where he is not made to live. These evils can be corrected only by a removal of the cause.

The cause of economic enslavement has been indicated by advanced students of Nature. They place the responsibility on the cold zone. August Engelhard wrote: —

"Winter has estranged us from Nature in every way. Under the scepter of winter, Nature is reversed, and the most unnatural becomes the most natural. It turns men into beasts, making them eagerly eat the steaming corpses of dead animals, to fill with warmth the body that is shivering with cold. It makes men wear the heaviest and thickest clothes — coffins for our bodies. It forces men to dig out stone and iron from the bowels of the earth to build strong houses for protection from the bitter cold. For the same reason it compels men to use fire and light, artificial nourishment — in short, to lead an artificial life.

"It has made artificial men of us, who have to struggle for substance, for all these unnatural wants, which are, in fact, nothing but nails in our coffins. Artificial dolls, working at their coffins — that is what man of yesterday and of today are out of the tropics." (*New Gospel,* page 26).

The subject before us is of paramount importance and involves all the various angles of Life Science. It must be considered in a scientific manner.

The highway of Health and Longevity is governed by Law, and that Law is the object of our search.

The findings of every investigation clearly show that our goal lies in the warm regions of the earth.

The Ancient Masters considered the Sun as the Savior of the World. That Sun is not a man. It is the glorious globe of heat and light that keeps the earth from being a barren waste of ice and snow.

These Masters also worshiped the Sun as the Grand Power that supplies the heat which is required to transform Potential Being into Actual Being.

We saw that an egg contains a potential chick, but heat must be applied to the egg to activate the Life process that transforms the potential chick into an actual chick.

That seems very simple to us because the knowledge is so common. But right there lies the secret of actual physical being.

Life is omnipresent, and potential being is omni-prevalent. But the heat of the Sun is required to activate the Life Principle and transform potential being into actual being. That principle is universal.

This scientific knowledge guides us to the Tropic Zone, the Kingdom of the Sun, and the only region of the earth that meets all the requirements of Life Science.

This scientific knowledge guides us to the Tropic Zone, the Kingdom of the Sun, and the only region of the earth that meets all the requirements of Life Science.

A valuable work on this subject, by August Beathman and August Engelhard, was published by the late Benedict Lust. From this work the following is excerpted by permission:

1. Greatest height of the Sun, vertical sun-rays in the tropics, consequently the largest amount of energy from the sun.

2. Greatest strength and light-power of attraction of the sun. The graceful beings of the animal and vegetal kingdoms could not have been created without it.

3. Greatest speed of rotation of earth on its axis, consequently the strongest centrifugal force and smallest centripetal force.

At the equator occurs the fastest motion of the earth, while the revolutions are very slow at the poles. No point of the earth's surface is so far from its internal center as the tropical belt; therefore, the pull of centripetal force is weakest in this belt, making man feel lighter on his feet and freeing his body more from the damages resulting from the strong, downward pull of centripetal force, erroneously called "gravity."

The smallest centripetal force and the strongest centrifugal force make all objects lighter in weight and they feel less the weight of their bodies. Walking is easier and man feels a sense of lightness on his feet.

Greatest order, regularity, and ability of distinction in every respect regarding climate, processes, as animal and vegetal growth.

Man, the most orderly and regular being so far as mind and body are concerned, could originate only in the tropic zone, and there only can he maintain himself at his best.

Smallest difference in seasons; no dark, cold weather. The cold and darkness of winter are an ally of death. Winter makes man inhabit houses and cover himself with clothes, all of which are enemies of health and life.

Smallest variation of temperature between day and night. In the tropics at certain altitudes there is no excessive heat in the day nor chilling cold at night.

Smallest difference in length of day and night. At the poles the days and nights are each six months long. In the tropics only slight variations occur in length of days and nights all thru the year.

In a region with small variations in temperature and in length of day and night, man will develop properly in harmony with his environment. He will have better constitution and body organization than those living in colder regions.

Our religion and civilization are based on the work of the Ancient Masters who dwelt in the tropic and semi-tropic regions. Man cannot develop his mental powers when forced to fight for life against the oppressive elements of a hostile environment.

Evergreen, richest vegetation on earth makes the best air for man to breathe.

Green and growing vegetation inhales and purifies the deadly vapors exhaled by man and animals. In the cold zone in winter, when vegetation is dormant, trees naked and barren, this vast, natural system of air-purification is not operating, making air worse in winter than in summer. That is another reason why tropical natives have excellent lungs, large chests, with freedom from coughs, colds, influenza, pneumonia, and all ailments of the respiration organs.

Highest development of animals and therefore the most man-like-the monkey family,

Monkeys are also children of the Sun. Like man, they cannot live in the cold zone without an artificial environment to protect them from hostile elements, just as they degenerate and die early under artificial conditions, so do man.

The most highly developed and most nutritious plants — the nut-and-date bearing palms. also the mango, avocado, banana, and pineapple.

Smallest consumption of food, no clothes nor houses necessary; in a word, absence of want and poverty.

Temperate zone or tropics; land of winter blizzards or land of eternal spring and light. — A Carefree Future.

Chapter No. 5
The Artificial World

"The Environment born of our intelligence and our inventions is adjusted neither to our stature nor to our shape. We degenerate morally and mentally. The natural conditions of existence have been destroyed by modern civilization. In truth, our civilization has created conditions of existence which render life itself impossible." (Carrel in *Man, The Unknown*).

Who can be so foolish as to expect Health and Longevity in an Environment composed of "conditions of existence which render life itself impossible"?

But science expects it. Moreover, that science freely spends millions of dollars annually on attempts to find remedies to suppress the aches and pains produced in man's body by the "unnatural conditions of existence which render life impossible."

Can that be considered the work of intelligent men? Was any human effort ever more foolish or worthless? Was the set of man ever engaged in a task more stupid and hopeless? Was any system of "science" ever more unscientific or preposterous?

While medical art appears to ignore the fact, everything in the Universe is ruled by law. Accordingly, the treasures of the earth become ours, including Health and Longevity, as we learn and apply the law of their production. Man may have anything he wants if he supplies the conditions to produce it; for he reaps what he sows *(Galatians 8:7)*. God has put beyond his reach nothing that he should have.

When man moves into an Environment with a health standard above his own, his health begins to improve, provided his habits are good. This fact is often demonstrated and definitely was in the case of the group that went from this country to tropical Panama in 1934, where they not only built a condition of good health, but have not been sick since. A poor place for doctors.

The law works both ways. When man moves into an Environment with a health standard below his own, his health starts to decline no matter how good his health habits, and continues to decline until his health standard falls to the low level of that of the Environment.

In the Temperate Zone man has built an Artificial World in which he grows many kinds of vegetables in winter, including plants that naturally grow only in the tropics.

Man appears not to realize that, corresponding to this Artificial World of glass for his plants in winter, he has also built an Artificial World to protect himself from the killing cold.

But the health and life of his plants seem more valuable to him than his own. He knows the plants must have much sunlight or they will die, but he seems to forget that his own body is ruled by the same law.

His own artificial world consists of dark stores, dark offices, dark factories, and dark houses. In the latter he leaves a few openings to let in the light, then covers them with shades to exclude the light so it will not fade his rugs and wallpaper. These also are more valuable than his own health and life.

In the unnatural darkness of that artificial world, the plants would soon perish, man lives and labors thru the years, hidden from the vitalizing sunlight, excluded from the energizing outside air, breathing over and over again the toxic fumes of his artificial world, his body filled with ailments, their cause a "mystery" to the doctors, and the doctors thriving on his misery and misfortunate.

It requires a strict social pattern and a rigidly controlled mind to keep man in darkness as to the dangers of his environment.

It requires little intelligence or common sense for one to realize that good health and long life are impossible in that artificial world.

Carrel declares that civilized man is without protection from the dangers of the hostile conditions of his Artificial World that he has built so he may live a short, miserable life of aches and pains in a land where he is a stranger.

That being the unbiased findings and conclusions of one of the great doctors of modern times, no one could even expect to have good health while living under "conditions of existence which render life itself impossible."

As a hostile environment is not capable of adjusting itself to the stature, shape, and requirements of the human body, the adjustment must be made to prevent sudden death; it is made by the body itself, at the expense of its vitality. Thus the body constantly grows weaker as it strives to live where it is not made to live.

Few doctors know how the body adjusts itself to an evil environment and evil habits. The first smoke makes the youth sick. He disregards the warning and continues. The deadly nicotine soon weakens the nerves sufficiently so that the body is unable to protest, and it sinks into degeneracy — the adjustment thus becoming so complete that the body in time craves the very poison it first rejected.

That is an example of the work of Vital Adjustment. Were the body's constitution so inflexible that such adjustment could not occur, there would follow such a violent swaying of vital activities from one extreme to the other that the force of the shock would cause sudden death — and it often does.

As a rule, death comes not suddenly in these cases. It creeps upon the unsuspecting victim by slow degrees — dying by steps and stages of 'disease' while paying the doctor thru the years to do what you think he can do, but what he knows he can't do.

The Process of Vital Adjustment comes into action at birth. The body, sound and vigorous when born, begins its painful adjustment to the evils of its environment.

The symptoms of the adjusting process in action are badly misunderstood by medical art. They appear in a series of illnesses called "children's disease," and are given misleading names — croup, whooping cough, mumps, measles, diptheria, scarlet fever, etc.

There are no children's diseases. In fact, there are no diseases. The Sun does not rise. What the world knows as "diseases" are but the symptoms of the degenerative process in action, as the health standard of the body declines to the low level of that of the environment.

Now perhaps you understand what Carrel means when he said "our civilization has created conditions of existence which render life impossible." Under the evil influence of his environment man sinks down and dies by inches.

In the case of infants and small children, polluted air appears as the worst enemy because they stay indoors most of the time. Some infants die in their cribs from breathing air polluted in the home. Caged birds never live long in such air.

Vital statistics of the nation show that ailments of the breathing organs are the chief cause of death in children up to their tenth year. Before children are five years old, their lungs show so much damage done by polluted air that it can be detected by x-ray.

There is evidence of degeneration in the child at the age of five or less. The health standard of the little boy has been lowered by polluted air, and the body sinks into a process of decline long before man has grown.

If the health conditions of the environment met the requirements of the body, sickness could not occur in the absence of bad habits. An infant has no bad habits and should never be ill unless overfed by foolish mothers.

Up to their tenth year, children develop no bad habits of their own accord. Parents, environment, and doctors are responsible for all sickness of such children.

Man is what his environment makes him, says Carrel, and the making process begins at birth. He cannot control and cannot rise above the health plane of his environment. He is slowly and constantly being molded into a condition of weakness and decrepitude by the health destroying agencies of his environment. The leading one is polluted air.

Polluted air is the only external element of Man's environment which can injure him and which he cannot control. To injure him, it must enter his lungs and filter into his blood, nerves, and cells. That it surely does with each breath.

It is shown by investigation that in the large cities fully 69,000 particles of various kinds of poisonous filth, grime, acids, dust, carbon, etc., enter man's lungs every time he breathes. That is several times a minute. His body is literally made of these poisonous substances and, as a result, it is filled with aches and pains, chills and fever. His lungs turn black from their natural color of pink and grey. The surprise is not that this man dies so young, but that he lives so long.

Man's body is but a mass of condensed air. The water he drinks and the food he eats are compounds of condensed air. So is the earth itself.

From the air come all things, even man's strength, vitality, and life. He becomes a living soul only as air flows into his lungs *(Genesis 2:7)*. When he stops breathing, he stops living.

From birth to death civilized man lives in a sea of polluted air. No element of his environment damages him so much as polluted air.

While science shows that civilized man is surrounded by destructive influences, the Doctors find no profit in the study of them and know little about the remarkable powers of the body to adjust itself to the evil influences, habits, and conditions which the body cannot control. Medical art takes too much for granted.

The Law of Vital Adjustments, or Vital Accommodation, is termed Nature's Balance Wheel by some biologists.

The power of vital adaptability is one of the ever-present facts of living existence. But for this power the smoker and drug addict would drop dead in a few days.

This is the law that prolongs life and permits the victim to drag out a miserable existence of aches and pains, erroneously called diseases. These acnes and pains, chills and fever, are the symptoms of the degenerative process in action. When the victims go to early graves, the basic cause is never suspected.

Man lives under all sorts of health-destroying conditions and forms all kinds of bad habits. If he has any good habits, he must apologize for them because of their unpopularity. These victims would drop dead more often than they do, but for the saving power of the Law of Adaptation.

When a healthy man goes to live and labor in an environment with a poisonous atmosphere, the little understood process of the body's adjusting itself to its environment comes into action automatically. There is a sneeze, then a cough, then a cold. Then appear more serious symptoms of chills and fever, influenza and pneumonia, etc.

Right before your eyes we see the adjusting process by which a hostile environment brings down to its level the condition of the body.

Such a man does not die suddenly, but lives only because the Law of Adaptation automatically comes into action. But the ailments weaken him. He comes back slowly. The sicker he is and the more of the doctor's poisons he takes, the slower he comes back.

How far back does he come? Every man can remember that last sickness which left a weakness from which he never entirely recovered. The weakness each illness left before that was definite, but too faint to be noticed.

No one ever comes back completely from any illness, no matter how slight. If one did, one would never know decrepitude, would never suffer somatic death, and would live forever in the flesh.

Every wound and every ailment leaves its scar. Carrel says, "Each illness has definitive consequences. We bear forever the scars of these events." (page 170).

There is and must be "perfect correspondence" between the body and its environment. That condition is produced by a series of illnesses which cause degenerative changes within the body. Thus the vital body of youth is slowly weakened and dragged down to the corresponding health standard of its environment.

The adjustment does not occur suddenly. There is no sudden swaying of vital function from one extreme (good health) to the other (sudden death).

When the organism's health standard is above that of its environment, Vital Adjustment comes into action, with the result that air so foul it nearly floored you when you first entered it, you will in time come to breathe without apparent inconvenience.

Never forget that a price is paid for that adjustment. Greene says, "such adaptation occurs only at the expense of a depression of all the vital functions, which must be permanently injurious if long continued or often repeated."

That "getting used to it" is the work of Vital Adjustment. The polluted air depresses the vital functions and renders them too weak to combat the danger with enough force to cause noticeable inconvenience.

The danger is still present. We may spray with disinfectants to kill offensive odors, or use "air wick or vaccinate and inoculate, and thus weaken the danger which the vital body does feel, the depressed, weakened, partially paralyzed body does not feel.

By making the body weaker when necessary, it will tolerate more abuse and poison and live longer under adverse conditions. A paradox too deep for medical art.

But for this automatic adjustment by degrees, it would be a case of violent swaying of vital function from one extreme to the other — sudden death.

This power of Vital Function and the operation of the Law of Vital Adaptation appear to have been unknown to Spencer. It is unknown to medical art, to the doctors, and to the multitude. To mention it brings only a smile. They pity your ignorance.

By the adverse effects of his environment and his bad habits, man's body is transformed, by a slow process of degeneration under the Law of Adaptation, from its perfect state at birth to that decrepit state termed Old Age provided he is lucky enough to live that long.

Chapter No. 6
The Art of Living

"No part of the Adamite period is more strongly emphasized than the warm climate of the Edenic World...Another thing, stated in language too plain to be misconstrued, is the great longevity of man in antediluvian days. People lived to be 800 and 900 years old. Man's physical Environment at that time simply impelled long life." (Professor L. N. Vail in *Earth's Annular System*).

Carrel finds that "our civilization has created conditions of existence which render life itself impossible," and cites some of these conditions as follows:

"The modern city consists of monstrous edifices and of dark, narrow streets full of gasoline (and thousands of other) fumes, coal dust, toxic gases (and acids), torn by the noise of taxicabs, trucks, and trolleys, and thronged ceaselessly by the great crowds (all persons more or less afflicted with some ailment and each exhaling terrible filth from his lungs). Obviously it (modern city) has not been planned for the good of its inhabitants." (*Man, The Unknown,* page 25).

There are the two pictures. Just as surely as Adam's healthful harmonious Environment impelled long life, that surely does man's modern Environment of discord and oppression degenerate his body and shorten his life.

It does not make sense to write a library of technical books in attempt to explain a problem so plain that it can be understood by a child and end that attempt by creating confusion and explaining nothing.

42

Vail agrees with advanced biologists that in the pre-flood period man's physical Environment was so perfect for him that it "simply impelled long life."

That evidence proves that man then fit his Environment and his Environment met all the requirements of his body. That is Spencer's Perfect Correspondence and the Fundamental Plan of Life.

Scientific living means living in harmony with the Law of Creation as it works in the direction of Construction. That leads to health and longevity.

Bad health, so-called disease, is the effect of transgressing the law and causing the Creative Process to work in the direction of Destruction as it strives to save the body from threatened danger.

The Creative Process produces nothing on the physical plane until the Conditions of Creation are perfect. When the Conditions become imperfect, the things created decline and decay, whether men, animals, or plants.

The science of living is as simple and certain as the science of corn production. The farmer knows all the requirements and proceeds accordingly, being certain of the results without "scientific advice." Before he prepares the land, he knows that when the weather is good, the soil is good and the seed is good, the crop will be good.

No guess-work; no speculation; all science. Good health is just as certain when the conditions of good health are present.

Living for health is not only a science, but an exact science. Nothing is left to accident and chance, to doctors and drugs, to tests and experiments. It involves not a study of medicine and disease, of rats and mice. It involves only a study of the conditions that produce good health.

The science of living is not subject to "progress." It does not change nor grow obsolete, but is always up-to-date. It is the same now as when man first came on earth and will be the same when the last man leaves. It is fixed, positive, and eternal.

We are purposely misled by propaganda about "progress." When we work with Cosmic Law there is no "progress." For "progress" means change, and Cosmic Law never changes.

What medical art calls "progress" means discarding a useless method for a new one which time soon proves to be no better. So the "progress" goes on and on and gets nowhere.

The race is progressing backward, from bad to worse. We must reverse the lever of living in harmony with the requirements of Cosmic Law, and all other good things come with improved health.

Medical art is not interested in that brand of science. For if it were applied to human life, it would destroy the sweetest racket on earth.

If man lived within the law, in the land where he is made to live, was never sick, and lived a thousand years, it would ruin all institutions that live and thrive on human misery.

While civilized man is surrounded by many destructive influences, medical art finds no profit in the study of them, consequently it knows little about the remarkable powers of the body to adjust itself to evil conditions.

Physiologists show that the human body is so perfect that it adjusts itself to the changing conditions of its Environment far better than the lower animals do. Were this not so, man's life-span would be still shorter.

Man lives in every climate, is subject to all kinds of evil influences, and indulges in every sort of habit. They are omnivorous, heedless, indulging daily in mineral, vegetal, and animal poisons on the supposition that they are food. The evidence is hourly before us that man may become accustomed to almost anything short of hanging. No matter how repugnant or destructive a thing naturally is, the body will take it and survive, provided time is given to secure the efficient operation of Life's Balance Wheel, whereby a violent swaying of vital activities from one extreme to the other is prevented.

The body saves itself from sudden death by its adjustment to evil conditions and evil habits. Instead of dropping dead, man dies by degrees. In that slowly dying process he suffers various ailments until his body can take no more and the grave ends it all.

Regardless of how well man lives or how good his habits, the condition of his body can be no better than the condition of his Environment.

Remove a fish from the water, its natural environment with which its being is in perfect correspondence, to dry land, and it soon dies because dry land is hostile to its being. It could not come into existence on dry land, neither can it live there.

That is an example of the power of Environment over living creatures. It is so simple that it can be understood by a child, it is definitely to the point.

Remove a fish from the stream and put it in a tub of water and see how soon it dies unless the water is often changed. Why? because the fish consumes the oxygen in the water and pollutes the water with the poisonous emanations of its body. That polluted water soon kills the fish.

Man lives all winter in the cold zone in a heated box where the killing cold makes adequate ventilation impracticable. The inside air is soon badly polluted with the fumes of cookery, may be with tobacco smoke, and the filthy emanations of his body and breath.

If man were no tougher than the fish, he would soon die in the polluted air of his home as the fish dies in the polluted water of its tub. He gets "used to it" because of the marvelous powers of adjustment of his body. But this power does not make man immune to his polluted Environment, and he dies by inches.

An adult poisons nearly a barrel full of air at each exhalation. That foul air he breathes over and over again all winter in his home. The results are colds, coughs, sore throat, mumps, measles, scarlet fever, chickenpox, small-pox, influenza, pneumonia — and early death.

Watch newspaper reports showing the great increase of these ailments during winter. Now you know why. It's all a mystery to medical art.

When the question is considered from the fundamental viewpoint, it is seen that the comparison is not overdrawn between a fish out of its natural home and man out of his. The analogy is perfect; the picture is astounding.

Certainly, man has the ability to do much better than the helpless fish. He is endowed with intelligence and power to do what the fish can't. He can build an Artificial Environment to serve as a poor substitute for his Natural Environment and, by so doing, can often manage to avoid extremely early death and may occasionally live a century, as some do.

Man was created mortal — a condition in which somatic death or eternal physical life was a possibility, depending upon his conduct whether he obeyed or disobeyed the Law. "Had he remained obedient," says Russell, "He would have continued living in the flesh until now — and forever — and yet all the while he had been mortal, liable to physical death if disobedient."

Various discoveries and experiments prove that eternal life in the flesh is a possibility; hence it is reasonable to suggest that man should have little difficulty in living a thousand years. The fact that the majority of men die under sixty-nine and only small minorities reach the century mark in civilization is proof that man is destroyed by a hostile environment and his own bad habits.

The condition of the body is modified, changed, by our Environment and our habits; and most of our habits, whether good or bad, are forced upon us by Environment, associates and conventionalism.

The human body possesses the potentialities of health and longevity. These potentialities become actualities only as the body lives and moves in the direction of Creative Construction. That involves good climate, good environment, and good habits.

These are the conditions in which the Creative Process works freely, naturally, without hindrance or obstruction. Under these favorable conditions it works in the direction of Construction, of Evolution, to an improvement in the species but not to a change of the species.

To the limit of its capacity and ability, the body adjusts itself to adverse changes and events instead of dying suddenly. Its organs improvise means of meeting practically every new condition to the extent of their capacity which, of course, is not without limit. Were that capacity unlimited, man could live without danger in any environment and under any conditions.

These physiological adjustments are such as tend to give man a maximum duration. Otherwise he could not live 75 or

100 years under conditions so hostile to his being that many men fail to reach the half century mark.

Under all conditions and at all times that watchful automatism called adaptation or adjustment makes possible man's existence under adverse conditions that he was never made to face.

The adaptive functions are working every moment of our life. They enable man to recover from illness in spite of the dangerous poisons the doctors inject into the body.

Chapter No. 7
He Lived 370 Years

"It is admitted that the poor toilers in our great centers (in the cold zone) deteriorate with each generation and if not revitalized by fresh blood (from more healthful regions) they become extinct in three or four generations." — (S. A. Strahan in the address before British Association for Advancement of Science; Densmore, page 380).

Modern man does not understand that in the cold zone he lives in the most artificial era that history records, or that humanity has known. Being the most artificial, it is the most dangerous to health and life.

As man leaves the Natural Life and replaces it with artificial conditions, he leaves health and longevity and replaces these with illness and early death.

The health problem resolves itself into an economic struggle in which the victors are those who strike off the shackles of economic slavery and become the masters of their destiny. Then only has man that glorious opportunity to live and do what he knows leads to health and longevity.

The presence of physical man on earth is the direct result of climatic conditions that made possible his physical being. If climatic conditions over the earth should change so greatly that physical man could no longer exist under them, he would disappear and become extinct as a physical being.

Were the entire surface of the earth now a frigid, polar region, it would mean the end of physical man as certain as the rising of the Sun.

It the entire surface of the earth at this time were a tropical region, flowing with fruits and flowers, man would again be in the Garden of Eden and have a life-span of nearly a thousand years.

The ages of certain ancient people are definitely recorded in chapters 5 and 11 of the Book of Genesis.

From Adam and Eve to Noah, the life span fluctuated but little and averaged 912 years. After Noah, for reasons now unknown, a rapid decline in the life span appears, and in eight generations it had dropped to 148 years, the age of Nahor *(Genesis 11:25)*.

Some authors attempt to show that the ages of the biblical patriarchs were computed in years much shorter than those of modern times. They go so far as to reduce the period three-fourths.

If the last assumption were correct, then Methuselah lived only 243 years, Nahor 37, and Abraham 44. Enoch would have been only 16 when he begat Methuselah, and Arphaxad less than 9 when he begat Salah, and Salah only 7 when he begat Eber. Adam would have been more than a great-grand-father at the age of 33.

It is written of Isaac that his age was "an hundred and fourscore years," and that he died, being "old and full of days" *(Genesis 35:28, 29)*.

Reducing Isaac's biblical age three-fourths, he had been only 45 at death — surely not an age that the historian could consider as old and full of days," when Isaac is but eleven generations removed from Noah, who lived 950 years.

While modern skeptics question the biblical ages of the antediluvian patriarchs, the Jews and other ancient races never doubted them.

Josephus gave a list of ancient authorities who believed that the early patriarchs did live nearly a millennium. In support of this view, he observed that their astronomical and geometrical discoveries could not have been made had they lived less than 600 years. This observation is supported by modern astronomical researchers.

Mr. M. Crommelim, of the Astronomer Royal Staff at Greenwich, wrote: "The period alluded to by Josephus consists of two of the most satisfactory cycles, that is 300 years, for the calculation of total eclipses. How the ancient astronomers became aware of these cycles seems now to be unknown."

The ancient Chinese have accounts of primeval extreme longevity in their records, most of which have been destroyed by despots to conceal certain facts.

The Chinese Emperor Ho-ang-to, who was shown by the chronology of China to have been contemporary with Abraham's great-great-grandfather Reu, who lived 239 years *(Genesis 11:2);* wrote a medical book in which he proposed the following inquiry:

"Whence it happened that the lives of their forefathers were so long compared with the lives of the then present generation," which had a life span of less than 300 years.

The ages of the early kings of Egypt and Babylonia were approximately the same as those of the biblical patriarchs.

A better explanation cannot be offered for the remarkable resemblance between the accounts of the duration of the reigns of the earliest Egyptian and Babylonian Kings and those of the biblical patriarchs, and that the accounts all refer to the same history of these ancient people.

The importance of the Egyptian and Babylonian list is that they indicate the longevity of the biblical patriarchs was a matter of common knowledge in both these countries.

The extreme longevity of the antediluvian patriarchs is an objection that seems to weigh heavily against the probability of historical accuracy as we trace back before the Flood.

Better knowledge of physiology has constrained the most-able of modern investigators to minimize that objection. For example, Doctor Fiossas, in his "Le Longevita Humaine," wrote:

"There is nothing in the human organs, in the function or in the properties of the body, to indicate their duration. It is neither contrary to reason, nor to the laws of the human organism, apart from unnecessary and incidental. Maladies that disturb its harmony, or extreme violence that injures its mechanism, that it should live for many centuries. The long life of biblical patriarchs is a fact more rational, more in accord with the present known laws of physiology, than is the brief existence of men who inhabit the earth today." (pages 346-7).

When the Europeans first discovered South America, they found that the natives of the tropical regions there had a life span of from 200 to 300 years, according to Sir. William Temple, quoted by John Smith in his *"Natural Food of Man."*

The press of May 22, 1955, reported that a man had born when George Washington was still President of the USA — the man lived in Colombia.

This man, Javier Pereira, was found by Douglas Storer, president of Believe It or Not, Inc., while on a flying trip through South America in search of unusual facts for Believe It or Not, which appears in the press.

The account says: "Indications are that Pereira is at least 150 years old, and probably as old as 166. An 86-year-old woman from his native village of Monteris remembers meeting him, already an old man, when she was still a child. Pereira himself, unable to read or write, relates events of the early 19th century, which indicates that he was over 21 at that time."

Pereira was given a physical examination at the San Vincente de Paul's Hospital in Medellin, Colombia, and the astonished doctors found that while his wrist joints and radial artery revealed extreme age, his blood circulation was that of a youngster.

The most conservative age estimate was given by Doctor Jose M. Restreps, an authority on human age who has met and treated several persons as old as 112, and he said that Pereira was older than 120.

The press of October 11, 1955, reported that a farmer in the Azerbaijan republic, bordering Iran, named Mahmud Fivozov, recently celebrated his 147th birthday. The radio broadcast said he had 23 children, including a daughter 120 years old.

The press reported the case of Li Chung-yun, of tropical China, who died in 1933 at the great age of 256. He buried 23 wives and at the age of 252 was lecturing to the students at the University of Chang-Fu. The biblical Peleg, but five generations after Noah, failed by 17 years to live as long as Li *(Genesis 11:19)*.

According to the press of 1923, Sadhu Swami, of Karimganj, India, was reported to be over 330 years old. He remembered events that occurred over a period of more than three centuries.

Peter Maffins, in his history of India, cited the cases of Numas De Cugna of Bengal, India, who died in 1566 AD at the age of 370. According to Ripley in his "Believe It or

Not," Cugna grew four new sets of teeth and his hair turned from black to grey four times.

Arphaxad, grandson of Noah, lived only 68 years longer than Cugna, dying at the age of 438 *(Genesis 11:13)*.

According to Homer, Nestor lived 300 years; and Dando, the Illyrian, passed the fifth century mark.

Dyson Carter recently wrote in The National Home Monthly that scientists now declare that it is well within the range of possibility for man to live 550 years.

Sixty and Seventy years ago the physicians of this country said that it was impossible for man to live a century and that all accounts to the contrary were false.

There are at this time still living several veterans of the Civil War which ended in 1865 — Ninety-one years ago.

Late Reports on Old People

The press of November 13, 1956, stated that Mrs. Laura Stantson, born in Slavery at LaGrange, Georgia, died the day before at the age of 106, leaving 52 grandchildren and many great-grandchildren.

The press of November 24, 1956, stated that Peter V. Ortiz of Anaheim, California, had just opened a bank account for old age. He was born in Lampazoa, Mexico, April 2, 1850.

The press of November 23, 1956, stated that Mrs. William Miller, of Hollywood, Florida, celebrated her 107th birthday the day before by entertaining some 75 of her 140 living descendants.

The press of November 14, 1956, stated that Mr. Walter W. William, forage master in Hood's Texas Brigade in the Civil War, had just celebrated his 114th birthday.

The press of October 22, 1956, stated that William Bisset, of Port Elizabeth, South Africa, had just celebrated his 160th birthday.

The press of 1956 carried many accounts of Javier Pereira of Columbia, South America, now 167 years old, who was brought to the United States to be examined by scientists to determine the cause of his long life.

The press of November 13, 1956, mentioned Mrs. Maria Garzon Ciuda de Castanede, also of Columbia, South America, who was born December 30, 1778, making her 178 years old.

The great Carrel wrote: "A man of 45 (in the United States) has no more chance of dying at the age of 80 years now than in the last century. ... This failure of hygiene and medicine is a strange fact. ... In spite of periodical medical examinations, and increasing numbers of medical specialists, not even one day has been added to the span of human life" (in the United States) (*Man, The Unknown,* page 178).

Keep these facts in mind when you read the usual medical propaganda on how progress in medicine is increasing the life span.

Chapter No. 8
Law of Change

The Cosmic Process of Production is perpetually in operation, building and destroying, and uses the same material over and over in its work.

"The dissolution of the World," said the Ancient Masters, "consists, in essence remains, and from it new worlds are formed by the Creative Power; and thus is the Universe dissolved and resurrected in endless succession" (Pike, page 607).

Under the Law of Change, all living formations are in a constant state of mutation, of dissolving and condensing, destruction and construction. They are incessantly vaporizing and solidifying in an endless circle of change.

As long as equilibrium rules the changing order, the living existence of the organism continues but comes to an end when the state of equilibrium fails.

This cosmic phase of Universal Transformation presents that fundamental principle in operation throughout the Universe, termed the Law of Change.

Many years ago, a wise old man, after a lifetime of study of the world and its ways, decided that the ruling principle of the Universe is change. Only change is constant and permanent, he opined; and to illustrate his point, he declares, "You never step twice into the same stream."

In the ancient Egyptian Mysteries, this Principle of the Cosmos was symbolized as Man crucified. The true and definite character of the Crucifixion Doctrine appears only in occult science, according to which it is a cosmic verity, and, as such, is subject to Cosmic Law.

In the Ancient Mysteries, this Cosmic Principle represented various phases of the Creative Process, but chiefly the constantly changing world, conceived by the World-Soul (the Pa) as the sequence of Creative Evolution, the self-engendering and self-dissolving process of Eternal Formation. It symbolizes the Universe as constantly changing in the course of dissolution and resurrection, incessantly dying and being born again, as the stream that appeared ever the same, yet is constantly renewed.

The Initiate was taught that this law applies as well to man as to the Universe, of which he is a part. Its process was strikingly illustrated in the Ancient Mysteries by the Transformative Principle symbolizing Man Crucified. That is the origin and the ancient meaning of Crucifixion.

Man is part of the Universe, and in him the Universe presents a complete microcosm. Man is a microcosm of the Macrocosm. All is in Man as the Ancient Masters declared.

Man is part of the Universe; and the Universe, as Man is "ever dying on the Cross of Life" the Cross being the Phallic Symbol of Man created by the Cosmic Union of the Male and Female elements. Thus, the Crucifix employed in the Mystic Dramas of the Ancient Mysteries was a symbol of the ever-changing Universe as well as the ever-changing body of Man.

We cannot consistently maintain that Man is an epitome of the Universe, and in the same breath contend that his body does not share, with the Material Universe, the same benefits that flow from the law of physical dissolution and physical resurrection.

Consistency of thought demands that we proceed in our course in a direct line through infinite time to infinite results. So we must hold that it is impossible for the human body to grow old, wear out, and break down as for the Universe itself to suffer that unscientific and impossible fate. That position is supported by every phase of the Cosmic Law of Physiology without a single exception.

Mathematicians do not record exceptions. Mechanical laws know no exceptions. The laws of the Universe are invariable, omnipresent, illustrative of the character of Cosmic Processes.

Biologists show that the Living Organism, no less than the Universe, is subject to the Law of Change — that fundamental principle which is intended by Cosmic Law to make, and does make, the Human Body as eternal and everlasting as the Universe itself. And while the organized body itself may disintegrate, its elements are as eternal as the stars.

The Human Body is in a constant state of integration and disintegration, incessantly "dying on the Cross of Life," symbolically, and at the same time having new birth, cell by cell and organ by organ.

The renewal process, not recognized by medical art, raises the Living Organism up to a much more exalted plane of existence than a man-made machine, which is subject to the law of wear because it is a finished product and possesses no authentic power of self-renewal, self-construction, self-resurrection, as symbolized by the Crucifixion.

This Cosmic symbol of the Ancient Mysteries was plagiarized and liberalized in the New Testament.

The principle of physical dissolution and physical resurrection, in constant operation in Man as in the Universe itself, literally places the Human Body, an epitome of the Universe and subject to the law, far beyond the influence of the element of Time and Law of Wear. In fact, these two factors, per se, have no more effect on the Human Body that on the Universe itself, as explained in our health science under Pathological Age.

It is preposterous to hold that such a perfect organism can either wear out or grow old, as it seems to do and as medical art claims it does. It is to all intents and purposes, according to the findings of physiologists, made to be immortal to go on forever.

That is the profound mystery of Man which the Crucifixion symbolized in the Ancient Mysteries — Immortality.

Physiologists support this ancient doctrine by declaring that it is much more difficult to explain why Man dies, than it is to show that he should live forever.

The dual processes of Creation in the Living Organism are technically termed anabolism (renewal) and katabolism (dissolution). For want of better terminology, they may be described as physical birth and physical death. Anabolism is constantly bringing the body into being, and katabolism is constantly taking it out of being by dissolving its tissues into their original elements. The sum of these changes is termed Metabolism (Equilibrium).

Both processes are the physiological phases of Creation. The orderly dissolution of the tissues into their original elements is as much the work of the creative process as is the orderly construction of those elements into cells and tissues, blood and bone, nerve and brain. Both processes are ruled by a law that never varies.

These dual processes are constantly in operation in the living organism. Every cell in the body is constantly being replaced. The entire body is literally taken apart, cell by cell, and a new body is constantly being constructed cell by cell.

Every second of life man witnesses a new receiving, appropriation, and giving back — decrepitude and re-juvenescence revolving round each other continuously, dissolution destroying over and over again, and construction ever building anew.

Physical growth indicates that the constructive process exceeds the destructive process, until maturity is reached. Then in adulthood they become equalized and perfect equilibrium (metabolism) should prevail. If this balance of anabolism and katabolism were not disturbed, good health would never end. When it is, trouble arises, and the creative process instantly attempts to reinstate it.

Here is the point where good health ends. Now appear certain symptoms as the creative process strives to restore the balance between anabolism and katabolism. These symptoms are what medical art studies and falsely terms "acute Disease."

As to this Szedely writes, "There is a single disease — in harmony, whose symptoms are variously manifested, depending on the extent and mode in which natural law has been violated. This is the law of disease. There is a single health — harmony, which is manifested in permanent evolution towards perfection, in proportion as we are able to create and utilize the preconditions or existence in harmony with the laws of Nature." — Basis of Cosmo-therapy.

When the body's equilibrium is disturbed, there is a definite cause for it. Such things do not just happen. The cause must be determined and removed to restore equilibrium (health).

Who shall attempt to do it? The physician of course. But he is not competent to do it because he is not taught how to do it. Also, his lack of knowledge of the body's physiology is so complete that his ignorance has been proclaimed down through the centuries. Carrel repeats the proclamation in these words:

"In fact, our ignorance (of the body's functions) is profound. ... Immense regions of man's inner world are still unknown. ... We lack almost entirely a knowledge of the physiology of the nerve cells. ... An endocrinologist, a psychoanalyst, a biological chemist are equally ignorant of Man." (*Man, The Unknown,* pages 4, 289).

So the physician and surgeon, being ignorant of the body's physiology begins with his treatment and remedies to interfere with, not to aid, the body's functions. The cemeteries of the land are gruesome witnesses that testify to the sad results of this man's bungling and damaging work.

So far as its textbooks are concerned, medical art has not yet discovered that the entire structure of the body is in a state of continuous change. The body one has today is the same in shape, but not in substance, as the body one had last year. Even one's bloodstream completely changes in seven hours, and the body itself is completely renewed in from one to seven years.

In commenting upon the renewal process, Doctor Carrington writes: "The moment the last morsel of food is digested and the stomach is empty, a general reconstruction process begins; a new tissue formation owing to the fact that the broken down cells are being replaced by (new) healthy ones — which is Nature's method of repairing any destroyed or injured part of the organism.

"This replacement of cells means gradual replacement of tissues; replacement of tissues means that a new stomach has been constructed — a stomach in every sense of the word NEW — as new as is the filling in of wounds or between the fractured ends of bones" (*Vitality, Fasting, Nutrition*, page 490)

Anatomists and physiologists are not agreed among themselves to the length of time required to renew all the body structures; but seven years is the maximum estimate. Carrington thinks this time limit too long. He says:

"Since the present modes of living are monstrously abnormal and our bodies are, consequently, distinctly abnormal in composition and function throughout our lives, it follows that all such changes will be abnormal also and that the length of time occupied in all such changes is, at the present day and under existing conditions, entirely abnormal.

"It is my contention that, were cell changes not stunted and at times almost checked by the almost entire monopoly of the vital forces for the purpose of digestion and elimination, it could be definitely ascertained that the body changes with the seasons, as does the snake's skin; and I look for the not too distant day when science shall prove this to be a fact — by the observation of normal people instead of diseased ones — the method now in vogue" (pages 491-2).

Carrington exhibits undue optimism when he says he "looks for the not distant day when science" will be observing and studying "normal people."

Here as elsewhere, medical art has taken the present degenerated condition of the body as standard of health, instead of realizing that our present condition is both artificial and abnormal (ab initio). Hence the erroneous theories of health; also, the lack of appreciation of the fact that the man in civilization is more or less degenerated, and a large majority of men more or less demented.

It is upon this false-stated foundation that deductions are drawn by medical art from a study of more or less degenerated organisms that all such calculations as the above are based.

If the present rate of cell replacement is abnormal, it is only reasonable to suggest that statistics, such as the above, are calculated from erroneous premises and are wrong.

Every fact, of physiology, shows that the length of time would be much reduced in cell replacement since the less food eaten and the simpler the quality, the more chance has vital force to replace and renew disintegrated cells.

Observations of the phenomena of fasting have thrown a flood of light upon this subject and produced a number of most suggestive facts which were unascertainable by and hidden from those who have never observed cases of protracted fasts either in others or in themselves.

Certain physiologists hold that were cell change not hampered by the almost entire monopoly of the vital forces in the work of digestion and elimination, it could be definitely ascertained that the entire body, down to the biggest bone, changes with the seasons.

Granting that cell change may be thus sided, by adopting a simple and frugal diet, so that the entire body is renewed in one year instead of seven, it appears possible, while one is on an absolute fast, to effect the complete change within a couple of months.

From what we know of the rapidity of elimination, purification and tissue changes during a fast, physiologists contend that practically the entire body would have been replaced with new tissue in that time under this strict regime.

No matter how long man lives, when he dies his body is only seven years old according to the longest period set for its complete renewal.

Chapter No. 9
Fountain of Youth

"It was quite common that time to find people thousands of years old. In fact, they did not know death." — Baird T. Spalding.

Under the Law of Change, the human body is in a constant state of mutation, of dissolution and construction, as stated by Doctor Dalton. This dual process requires the aid of a transportation system, and that is present in the form of vascular system, described in our work "Breath and Blood," which the student should read.

The Ancient Masters knew that the River of Living Water incessantly flows thru the body. Ancient science discovered that secret of physiology thousands of years ago *(Genesis 9:4)*. Medical art knew nothing about it until 1616 A.D. and, when told of it, refused for forty years to believe it.

The Masters concealed their wisdom and discoveries in allegory and symbol to preserve them from destruction by despots. So it came to pass that the Ancient Greeks, unable to interpret the allegorism and symbols, believed that the arteries of the blood system were air tubes because they found them empty in the dead body and named them artere from "air."

In Harvey's day, this erroneous theory ruled medical circles. When his discovery of the blood circulation exploded the theory, the Holy Medical Authorities were content at first to ridicule him as a quack, a crackpot. When they at least realized that they were unable to disprove his statements, they were filled with rage and organized a system of persecution that soon drove him into exile. Then they confiscated his property, and Harvey died of a broken heart

Today the orthodox doctor who is so unethical as publicly to announce discoveries that explode medical theories is quickly silenced, his medical license revoked, and he is liquidated.

Forty years after Harvey announced his discovery, the medical world admitted that he was right. The arteries did not carry air as medical art had taught. They were tubes filled with blood during life but empty after death because the nerve force in the tubes is so strong that, in death, it drives all the blood from the arteries into the veins.

This fact proves that blood movement is independent of heart action. The blood flows in the arteries after the heart stops. Another medical theory exploded.

These facts of physiology were known to the Ancient Masters, as proven by their writings. But their secret knowledge of these facts was confined to their Mystery Schools and imparted only to those worthy to receive it. It was unknown to the masses. That accounts for the reason why such ridiculous theories regarding the physiology of the body prevailed from Aristotle (384-322 BC) till the time of Harvey (1578-1657 AD). Such theories still fill medical textbooks.

Down to the 17th century AD, medical art believed that the purpose of breathing was "to draw air into the body to cool the blood," and that the heart was a "furnace" from which came the "animal heat" of the body. That same medical art is engaged now in "combating disease" when there is none to combat.

From these preposterous theories rose the old Galenic doctrine (131-210 AD) that the "air introduced into the body by breathing served to regulate, to maintain and at the same time to temper, refrigerate the innate heat of the heart." As medical art drops these theories the action is called progress to deceive the people.

Again, the respiratory action of the thorax, according to Galen, "introduced into the blood the air that was necessary to generate the vital spirits in the heart."

Traces of this ignorance still appear in the medical theory that "food combustion" within the body produces heat, energy, brain, and nerve action, and these combined, according to physical science, are what we call Life.

"Life," wrote the great Osler, "is the expression of a series of chemical changes" (*Modern Medicine 1907, volume 1,* page 39).

That which is so boastfully proclaimed as "medical process" is the scrapping of these absurd theories which ruled medical art in the days of Harvey and were too intricate even for him to unravel. It was not until the last years of the 18th century that some of these silly theories were exploded by better knowledge of the body's physiology.

It was more than a century after Harvey, before Medical Art knew much about the body's physiology, and it knows but little now. The great Carrel wrote: "In fact, our ignorance (of the body) (and its functions) is profound." (*Man, The Unknown,* page 4).

It was not until the researches of Metchnikoff, Carrel, Crile, and others that medical art had any definite knowledge of the basic reasons why the human body grows decrepit and goes to the grave long before it should.

At this time medical art admits that it is still more difficult to explain why a man dies than it is to show that he should live forever.

Doctor Foissac declared that "the long life of the biblical patriarchs is a fact more rational, more in accord with the known laws of physiology, than is the brief existence of the men who inhabit the earth today." (Part II, Chapter 2).

In the light of these notorious facts, the shouting we hear about "medical science" and medical progress is the most preposterous prattle ever invented.

Before Harvey's discovery, medical art knew nothing about the physiological process of cell dissolution and cell replacement constantly occurring in the body, and it knows very little now. It knew not that the Bloodstream is a River of Living Water by means of which gases were conveyed from the lungs to the billions of body cells and also by which the poisonous substances produced by cell dissolution are carried off and disposed of thru the eliminate channels. It knows not how that the blood per se nourishing nothing. That is not, technically speaking, a stream of nutrition, but a system of transportation, as a railroad that carries farm products to cities for use as food and carries off the garbage, which we explained in our work entitled Breath and Blood.

Medical art knows not that the body is endowed with the power of Perpetual Youth; that the Fountain of Youth is a physiological process that keeps the body young in years regardless of the number of times a man celebrates his birthday. It rejects with scorn the suggestion of the possibility of physical rejuvenation. Yet that process is perpetually at work in every cell and tissue of the body.

Rejuvenation means becoming young again, as we explained in our work entitled *Scientific Living*. That actually occurs to a marked extent when man, at the ages of 28, 37, 40, and 79, are given up by orthodox doctors are incurable wrecks, and these broken men, seeing the light, turn to Mother Nature and experience REJUVENATION to such an extent that they recover their health and live more than a hundred years, outliving by many years the physicians and surgeons who told them that they could not get well and had but a short time to live.

Unto this day medical art has failed to give due consideration to the fact that the blood is a vast transportation system with several functions. It carries material for new cells to replace those in process of disintegration. As the Vital Stream is composed of what man breathes, drinks, and eats, the condition of his blood is within his control.

For ages the Ancient Masters had this basic knowledge and used it to rejuvenate their body and prolong their days. By their own work they proved their amazing wisdom. They lived thousands of years; and their somatic demise was a voluntary act, as we have explained elsewhere.

The chief object of medical art is not known as human betterment but its own preservation and perpetuation. It cares nothing about the Fountain of Youth, terming such theories nonsense and makes no attempt to recognize it. It hides its ignorance in the darkness of a dead language, and the multitude is mesmerized by what it cannot comprehend.

Before Harvey's discovery, medical art had no fundamental principle upon which to base any attempt to improve human health and prolong life. Out of his discovery came the knowledge that has led to some progress in this field. But the body's physiology is still so little understood that no doctor is yet qualified to direct properly the Process of Rejuvenation.

The Blood

The body of the average adult contains 10 to 12 pints of blood; and the blood system of the body may be compared to a water system that supplies the home with fresh water and the sewer system that carries off filth and waste.

With every heartbeat the blood, returning to the central blood station from all parts of the body, is sent to the lungs for purging and purification; and every second of time the purified stream flows back to the heart and then from the heart out over the body thru the aorta.

In the air cells of the lungs the blood receives from the air its load of oxygen, nitrogen, and other elements to sustain the body: and, at the same time, like a scavenger or a sewer system, the blood collects the body waste, in the form of gases and fluids, and eliminates this poisonous cargo thru the bladder as fluid and thru the lungs and skin as vapor and gases.

Nobody waste passes off in lumps and chunks. The waste does not pass off thru the bowels. The tissues merely disintegrate, forming liquids and gases, which leave the body as stated.

All that leaves the body thru the bowels is the residue of the food one eats. In the case of gluttons, this amount is considerable and several bowel movements are needed each day to dispose of the surplus food that the body can't use.

This surplus food forms useless fat, tumors, and other growths; and this shortens life. The average person consumes three to four times as much food as the body can use.

The largest item the body needs is oxygen. This gas is carried by the red blood corpuscles, each about 1/3200 of an inch in diameter. The blood contains 25 to 30 trillions of them. Their total combined surface is almost an acre — an acre approximately 210 feet square.

From the billions of air cells in the lungs, the Oxygen of the air we breathe, passes into the blood to be collected by the red corpuscles and carried to where needed.

When that Oxygen is polluted, as in city air, the corpuscles recoil from it because it is dangerous; and there, trouble starts. The remedy is good air, not drugs and nostrums, vaccines and serums. But if the masses knew that, medical art would become obsolete and doctors would be ruined.

The red corpuscles have a double concave surface and a smooth outline at their edges.

The absorption of polluted air into the blood thru the lungs causes rapid changes in these corpuscles. They lose their roundness becoming oval and irregular; and instead of having a natural attraction for one another and running together as they do in good health, they lie loosely scattered and indicate that he whose blood they were taken from is depressed and deficient both in muscular and mental tone.

The basic cause of this condition is unknown to medical art.

We are now down to the greatest cause of bad health known and unknown. In the 19th century, Doctor Parkes said that of all the causes of disease, breathing vitiated air is the chief. But as the remedy is good air and not drugs and nostrums, vaccines and serums, medical art was not interested.

The fine blood vessels of the lungs, called capillaries, lie in direct contact with the walls of the air sacs and are just big enough to allow the red corpuscles to pass thru them in single file.

During moderate activity, all the blood in the body passes thru the lungs more than 100 times an hour.

This means that each minute of life that vast corpuscle mass in our blood comes in direct contact with the vast air-sac-area of the lungs, to collect oxygen needed by the body.

All that separates the blood from the air in the air cells is a membrane about sixteen-one-hundred-thousand of an inch in diameter.

If the air we inhale is too warm, the blood vessels of the lungs expand, and the corpuscles are unable to pick up the oxygen so readily. That is one reason why very warm air is suffocating. Again, if the air is quite poisonous, the red corpuscles recoil from it, and that also produces suffocating sensations.

One reason why cool air is so bracing is because it is more condensed and contains more oxygen. There is more (25%) oxygen in zero air than in 100 above zero.

The symptoms of suffocating are not always the result of the conditions mentioned.

As the oxygen level of the blood falls below normal by reason of the oxygen being replaced by carbon monoxide gas, or for any other reason, there is not enough oxygen in the blood for the body's needs and symptoms of suffocation result.

The causes of distress within the body always come from without. They lurk in the person's habits and in the environment where he lives and labors.

If our habits were what they should be and our environment a healthy one, we would not be sick. That is the reason why the study of disease is a waste of time and money.

Doctors may study disease a million years, and they will end where they began.

Blood Purification

The term blood poison may frighten you; but in the process of living, your blood is poisoned thru and thru every 25 or 30 seconds of your life. It is and must be purified just as often.

The purification process occurs in the lungs. That is the only way the blood can be purified. It can be poisoned by drugs and nostrums, vaccines, and serums but never purified.

This subject is so important and so little understood by medical art that even the doctors are dying daily of disorders rising from blood poison.

The arterial blood flows from the heart into the body thru the arteries, and the same blood flows back to the heart thru the veins.

How does the blood get from the arteries to the vein? Thru the capillaries, a vast network of blood vessels connecting the arteries with the veins and so small that they could not be seen with the microscopes in 1616 when Harvey discovered the circulation of the blood.

For this reason, Harvey was unable to tell how the blood gets from the arteries into the veins, which means that in

Harvey's day medical art knew almost nothing about blood and body function. It knows but little more today, as it has no law of Psychology, Biology, or of Physiology.

The extreme smallness of the capillaries, with their exceedingly thin walls, is more evidence to expose medical ignorance and explode the medical theory that the heart is a pump.

If the heart acted as a pump to propel the blood in the body, it would have to force the blood, against the pull of gravity, from the feet up to the heart. The back pressure of this large mass of blood would fall on the thin walls of the tiny capillaries, which would result in the whole capillary system below the heart being ruptured and busted.

The blood capillaries in the lungs are the passages thru which the stream of Living Water flows for fresh air.

The billions of capillaries in the lungs wind among the tiny air tubes and twine around the air cells, as a vine among the branches and leaves of a tree. The walls of these little breathing organs of the capillaries are much thinner than the walls of soap bubbles. So, it is the slightest film that separates the air from the blood.

It is here that the air and blood intermingle, and here that the poisons and impurities of the blood, brought from all parts of the body, are cast off. It is here that a fresh supply of oxygen, nitrogen, sunlight, and all the other elements in the air that sustain the body and preserve its integrity are absorbed by the blood and carried to all parts of the body. This exchange of gases from the blood and gases of the air is so important that the slightest interference with it means Death, and it may be surprising to know that medical art pays little attention to it. That is another reason why so many people today are dropping dead of "heart attack."

When you stop breathing you stop living, no matter how good may be the condition of your heart.

The network of blood capillaries in the lungs are distributed everywhere in the minute spaces between the billions of air vesicles and envelope their walls within a vascular screen.

The blood flows thru the lungs in billions of small currents, almost in direct contact with the air in the lungs. In fact, it is as though the River of Living Water were sprayed thru a Breath of Life in an exceedingly fine shower of Red Mist so that every particle of Blood and every particle of Air in the lungs are brought together in the closest possible proximity.

1. The blood, from all parts of the body, goes to the heart and then directly to the lungs thru the right and left pulmonary arteries, the only arteries in the body that carry venous blood.

2. This blood flowing from the heart to the lungs is of a dark blue color, approaching to black.

3. This is venous blood and is saturated thru and thru with all the filth, waste, pollution, and poison collected from

all the cells, tissues, organs, glands, and blood vessels of the body.

4. The blood is now a filthy stream of poison in the broadest sense of the word, flowing to the heart thru the great veins from all over the body to be sent on to the lungs for renovation and purification. Unless the process of purification occurs quickly, without undue interference, death soon ensues.

5. As the purging process occurs in the lungs, a marvelous change occurs in the color of the blood. At the very instance that the poisonous blood passes into the air-cells, a lightning change takes place between the blood and the air, in which the color of the blood becomes a brilliant scarlet, due to the passage of the poison in the blood into the air-cells of the lungs, and eliminated and expelled as invisible vapor in the process of exhalation.

6. This process of Blood Purification, by which the blood exchanges its poisonous gases for the air gases in the lungs, occurs approximately 2,880 times every 24 hours, in which time approximately 125 barrels of blood are purified daily in the lungs.

Now you see why it is so important to know the condition of the air you breathe. If you live and labor in the polluted air of the city, that is the kind of air gases the blood must take up in the lungs, and that is the kind of air in which city dwellers live.

That fact shows that Doctor Parkes was right in the 19th century, when he declared that of all the causes of disease, breathing vitiated air is the chief.

And those diseases medical art attempts to "cure" by the use of other poisons in the form of drugs and nostrums, vaccines and serums, while paying little or no attention to the kind of air people breathe."

Blood Poison

In the polluted environment of civilization, where a breath of really pure air is not to be found, as the poisoned blood flows to the lungs for purification, there is simply an exchange of poisonous gases.

This is a condition of Blood Poison, and this condition must occur before you can have the slightest ailment — even the common cold. In 1923 we wrote a booklet on the subject, in which we said:

1. Astral Radiation is the creative force. In health it works smoothly and silently. When its function is obstructed, it struggles to save its Temple by removing the obstructing object or condition.

The surface symptoms of this internal struggle are what medical art calls "disease," giving them names according to the situs of the symptoms, and then treats the condition as though it were a destructive process. There is no such thing as disease per se.

2. The continuous and harmonious existence of the organism depends upon strict compliance with the Law of Life, written in every fiber of its structure.

3. The living organism, as a machine, is perfect and needs nothing but the greatest freedom to perform its work in harmony with the law.

4. The only healing power on earth is within the body itself and can be aided by nothing but by the body-sustaining agencies of the universe.

5. No force, no machine, no substance or thing, no drugs nostrums, vaccines, or serums are able to save the body or serve its healing power, further than to remove the cause responsible for its disturbed equilibrium.

6. The condition of the body depends upon the condition of the blood, and the condition of the blood depends upon the air we breathe, the fluid we drink, and the food we eat.

7. Insofar as the blood remains active and normal, and to that degree only, will and must all organs and parts of the body remain in health.

8. In direct ratio as the blood becomes stagnant, impure, and abnormal, will and must all organs and parts of the body decline from health. This is not disease but degeneration, with early death as the end of it all.

9. As the condition of the body depends upon the condition of the blood, it follows that good health or bad health depends upon and rises from the blood.

8. The River of Living Water that turns the Wheels of Life is not only the health-building and life-sustaining agency, but it is also the destructive power.

Therefore, the doctor worthy of the title is he who understands the Principles of Biology and Physiology, and he takes the following position:

> A. The condition of the body depends upon the condition of the blood.
>
> B. The normal flow of normal blood builds good health.
>
> C. Retarded circulation and polluted blood build bad health.
>
> D. Purification of the blood and acceleration of its circulation is scientific and effective treatment of bad health.
>
> E. The means to accomplish this purpose are supplied only by the body. Only the body makes blood and purifies it. Nothing else can do the work. The greatest chemist cannot make a drop

of blood; nor can he make any substance or concoction to improve the blood.

F. The source of supply determines the method of procedure.

G. The procedure must be natural and according to Cosmic Law. Then the results are and must be favorable and permanent.

Our language is simple and our explanations are clear because we realize that technical terms cannot be properly comprehended by 13-year-old minds, nor intelligently understood by more than 14% of the masses who are as a rule poisoned thru and thru with polluted air.

These figures on Mind and Brain Capacity are the scientific findings of psychologists.

If the best doctor on earth should study the subject of good and bad health for a century, he would come back to what has been said here about the blood and positively declare, there it is — it is all there.

This simple, understandable philosophy concerning the River of Life gives the reader a full and complete answer to that puzzling question, what is disease?

Rejuvenation

Harvey's discovery of the circulation of the blood revealed that the River of Living Water is the real Fountain of Youth. By its action, every cell of the body, every minute of time, is cleansed of the waste products of its work and kept in proper condition for its work.

This newly discovered secret medical art knows not how to use. The details of the procedure are unknown to medical doctors. Medical textbooks contain nothing on the subject. For the Holy Medical Authorities who wrote the books knew nothing of the secret. So the puzzled doctors of the rank and file slyly ask one another: "Why does the body seem to grow old and die? How can it wear out? Why does it not go on forever?"

When the great Metchnikoff answered these questions, he met the same jeers from his medical brethren that greeted Harvey when he announced his discovery of the circulation of the blood.

After years of investigation, Metchnikoff found that (1) deterioration of the body structure and (2) old age are (3) due to minute quantities of poisonous substances in the blood.

His book, *"Prolongation of Life,"* furnished the first logical theory in modern times of the degeneration changes occurring in the body and why. His findings have since been confirmed by leading researchers, including such prominent doctors as Carrel, Crile, and Empringham.

Crile said, "there is no natural death. All deaths from so-called natural causes are merely the end-points of a progressive acid saturation."

Empringham said, "All creatures automatically poison themselves. Not time but these toxic products (in the blood) precede the senile changes that we call old age."

Carrel asserted, "The cell is immortal. It is merely the fluid in which it floats that degenerates. Renew this fluid at proper intervals and give the cell proper nourishment upon which to feed, and, so far as we know, the pulsation of life (in the body) may go on forever. ... Quickly, involuntarily, the thought comes: Why not with man? Why not purge the body of the worn-out fluids, develop a similar technique for renewing them — and so win immortality" (in the flesh)? — *Man, The Unknown.*

Carrel was great, but he missed some vital points. He could not shake off the medical myth of cell nutrition.

We show in our work, *"Facts of Nutrition,"* that the body cells are composed of molecules, which are composed of atoms, which are composed of electrons, which are whirling centers of electricity and that in order to nourish the cell, we would have to nourish the component parts of the cell.

Nothing but Astral Force can nourish the cell because the cell is constituted of Astral Force.

Then why must man eat gross physical food? That question we have answered in *"Facts of Nutrition."*

Right in the attempt to nourish the body lies the error that hurries man to the grave. Feeding hastens the degenerative process, whereas fasting quickens the process of rejuvenation.

Carrel's experiments confirmed Metchnikoff's findings: That decrepitude and early death are due to poisons in the blood. Purge the blood of its poisons, said Carrel, and the blood becomes the flowing Fountain of Youth.

Carrel's experiments showed that when the fluids fail to carry off the excrement of the cells, they degenerate, become senile, and show signs of dying. Each time they were rejuvenated by a process of cleansing.

Here again Carrel missed a vital point. Body cells do not die, and he himself declared that they are immortal. The cells simply sink below the life-level of vibration because their magnetic poles become corroded by the acids that are not carried off and eliminated by a polluted bloodstream.

Patients recover quickly when fasting reduces the pollution in the blood, thus freeing the cells of the injurious action of the acids. That is also the process of rejuvenation.

This amazing knowledge leads physiologists to declare that old age and physical death, except by accident, are due to a polluted blood system and the accumulation of garbage. This results in corrosive magnetic poles of the cells, making them incompetent to receive the electric vibrations of the Life Principle, and they fall below the level of animation. That state we term death.

In his experiments with living cells, Carrel cleansed the cells of a chicken's heart by washing them in clean water. The cells of man's body are bathed and washed by the blood. If the blood is polluted, instead of cleansing the cells it pollutes them more.

Elimination is much more important than feeding. If blood purification by the kidneys were stopped, man would die in three to five days. If blood purification by the lungs were stopped, he would die in three to five minutes.

In the matter of health, we always come back to the blood. "It is merely the fluids in which the cell floats that degenerate," said Carrel, who added, "Why not purge the body of the worn out fluids, develop a similar technique for renewing them and so win immortality."

The secret of physical immortality seems to be that simple. That technique has been partially developed, and those who use it are ridiculed as quacks and crackpots by medical art.

By the process of fasting, the blood and body are cleansed and purged, provided man breathes pure air and drinks pure water. By fasting the balance of the blood is restored, and the body is rejuvenated provided the air and water that enter the body are pure.

The power that builds also destroys upon a reversal of the lever. The River of Living Water is replenished and renewed several times each day. But with what?

Here is the root of the problem. With every poison that man can inhale, drink, and eat does not kill him instantly the body receives its death-blow from the Vital Stream which the modern environment and man's habits have changed from the River of Health and Life to the Pool of Pollution and Death.

In due time, after much suffering, man dies "of a progressive acid saturation of his blood, cells, and tissues."

Chapter No. 10
Physiological Rest

Orthodox doctors constantly advise patients to "get more rest." But the rest that does the body the greatest good is that kind these doctors never heard of. It is physiological rest.

Doctor Charles W. De Lacy Evans wrote an extraordinary book titled *"How to Prolong Life."* In it he reviewed some 2,000 cases of those who had lived more than a century and summarized his conclusions in these words:

"We find one great cause that accounts for the majority of cases of longevity — moderation in the quantity of food eaten" (Densmore, page 295).

Evans found in the works of Plutarch that the ancient Britons "only began to grow old at the ages of 200 to 210; and their food consisted almost entirely of acorns, berries, and water." How many modern gluttons would exchange their diet for 100 or 150 years of life?

The Lancet of February 7, 1878, a London medical journal, reported the case of Miguel Solis, of San Salvador, half-breed Indian, who was then 180. The account said:

"Doctor Hernandez found this aged man working in his garden. He attributed his long life to his careful habits and to eating only once a day. He was accustomed to fast on the 1st and 15th of each month. He ate the most simple foods and took all things uncooked." (Densmore, page 297).

Doctor Arnold Lorand, in his work *"Old Age Deferred,"* wrote, "It is certain that more people die from the effects of eating too much than too little. It is surprising how little food man needs to live in good health." (page 280).

Doctor Sergius Morgulis, University of Nebraska Medical School, wrote a masterly work on the Value of Fasting. With precision instruments and equipment in his laboratory that constituted the last work of science in measuring physiological reactions, he produced clear proof in the course of years of patient work of definite facts which had long been known by the advocates of fasting.

Morgulis utterly exploded the medical theory that fasting is injurious. He established by an elaborate series of tests that a fast, continued until there is a loss of from 15 to 20 percent of body weight, is not only innocuous in many cases, but is usually highly beneficial.

One of the most interesting of all the lines of his investigation was his experimentation with hibernating animals.

The strange feature about hibernation is the fact that animals which spend the winter in this way are entirely without food for several months. The flame of life flickers just above the point where a further reduction of the vibratory rate would extinguish it, and the body temperature falls to practically the level of that of its immediate environment. But exactly what occurs in the body of a hibernating animal is at present unknown.

Morgulis mentions the Alaskan fur-seal bull "which neither eats nor drinks for about three months of the year or during the entire breeding season. This is remarkable, as the animals are at all times within easy reach of food."

Living in a state of great excitement, fighting off intruders, chasing mischievous bachelor bulls, keeping jealous guard of his "harem" of cows, the sexually hyperactive bull seal experiences an absolute fast so far as food and water are concerned, but his breathing must continue and does, or he would die.

By the middle of June, a majority of the full-grown bulls have established themselves on the beaches to await the coming of the cows. They seem to possess inexhaustible vitality. Many of the bulls have been on the beaches from the month of May; and from the time of their arrival to the early part of August, they touch neither food nor water.

From his experiments and investigation, Morgulis reached the conclusion that fasting is definitely a process of rejuvenation.

In order to explode again the medical theory that vitality results from food combustion in the body, in 1926 Bernarr Macfadden; then editor of Physical Culture, offered a cash prize of $1,000 to anyone who would walk without eating from Chicago to New York City.

In June-1926, George H. Johnson attempted the feat and was forced by sore feet to end his hike at Bald Knob, Pennsylvania on June 20. This is what he said:

"I hiked nearly 600 miles thru storm, wind, and sunshine, through burning heat and under innumerable difficulties, in twenty days and not a morsel of food passed my lips. ...

"When I reached the 500-mile mark, Macfadden notified me that I had won and was at liberty to end my feat of fasting. But I kept on. My mind urged me forward. My body was in fine shape, and the doctor with me said I was a great credit to the cause of fasting.

"But my tortured feet demanded rest. The tissues of my feet were worn away by the thousands of steps I had taken over burning pavements, and the delicate bones that form the arches were unprotected. This caused me excruciating pain, and at last I had to stop." (*Physical Culture,* August, 1926.)

Johnson's weight during the journey dropped from 157 pounds to 120. When his hike ended, his pulse was 60, body temperature 98, and blood pressure 101. The pain in his feet was so severe the last day of his hike that it required nearly thirteen hours for him to cover 19 miles, he said, "I hated to quit but it seemed best on account of my sore feet."

In spite of the many tests and experiments which conclusively prove that vitality is not the product of food combustion, the Holy Medical Authorities have made that theory their law of physiology in their textbooks, and no one dares to change it.

The press of August 6, 1937, said, "Invalid who fasted 104 days, reports self in good health. Former arthritis victim now plays badminton and dances instead of riding in a wheelchair."

The patient was Florabelle. Before her fast she was in a wheelchair, unable to walk; and her hands were so badly crippled she could hardly use them. She said, "For years I dragged around in pain and misery and wondered what people could find to smile about."

Mrs. Culbertson weighted 110 pounds when the fast began. At the end of 50 days of fasting, she weighed 90 pounds. Then she broke her fast for 40 days, and at the end of the 40-day eating period, her weight increased to 118 pounds. She fasted again for 54 days, and her weight dropped to 90 pounds. That made a total of 104 days out of 144 days without food. The account continues:

"Now, round and trim, she tips the scales at 120. Clear-eyed, vibrant, energetic, she enjoys her food, which consists mostly of fruits and vegetables. She regards as valuable experience her simple method of recovering her health."

For thousands of years, man has shown that the effects of fasting are definitely rejuvenating. There is nothing uncertain about the process. It works always in the same direction with good results. It would be calamitous for medical art if the multitude ever discovered the facts about the excellent results of fasting.

Experiments on lower animals prove without exception the detrimental effect of feasting and the beneficial effect of fasting. When alternately fed and fasted, they grew young again.

During the days of fasting, the worms were reduced to a fraction of their original size. When fed after the fast, they displayed all the physiological characteristics of young animals. Under continued feeding, they go again thru the process of growth and aging and may be made young again by fasting. That is the rejuvenating law of Nature and which medical art condemns.

With plenty of food, this species would pass thru its whole life history in three or four weeks. When alternately fed and fasted, they continue young and active for three years.

According to Julian Huxley, the extension of the life span of the worms in this experiment is equivalent in man to keeping him alive and active for approximately 3,000 years. Medical art regards as fiction the biblical account of Methuselah living 969 years.

In another experiment, Huxley fed a family of earthworms as they usually eat except one, which he isolated and fed the same way, but now and then he fasted it.

What happened? The worm alternately fed and fasted was alive and vigorous after nineteen (19) generations of its relatives had been born, lived their regular time, and died. Huxley explained the physiological secret of rejuvenation by asserting that heavy and constant eating clogs the life channels, decreases vitality, and hastens death.

Carrel found the same condition in his experiment with the living cells of chicken hearts. He discovered that when the blood is clogged with filth and unable to carry off the excrement of the cells, they degenerate, become senile, and show signs of dying. Each time they were rejuvenated by a process of cleansing.

Medical critics will assert that man is not a worm. But all living organisms are governed by the same Cosmic Law. The analogy between worm and man is legitimate. It is valuable in revealing the secret of Longevity.

The enlightening experiments with the worms show the dangers of being what doctors call "well nourished," When a worm is well nourished, it is on the way to early decrepitude and early death.

When worms are well fed, they grow fat. No doctor would condemn that; for it is the condition for which medical art strives. Feed children freely to make them grow fat and fast. That is the shortcut to the cemetery.

When the well-fed worms grow fat and fast, they reached maturity fast, they aged fast, and they died fast. But medical art would never attribute feasting and fast growth as being the cause of early decay and early death in man.

All tests show that eating is harmful to a certain extent, regardless of what one eats.

Two pens of rats were put on a feeding test. The rats in one pen were fed in a regular way and died in 650 days. The other rats fasted one day in three, and they lived 727 days.

Another test was made. It was termed "Studies in Underfeeding." If any doctor advised "underfeeding" he'd be considered crazy. People are warned by medical art that they must be "well nourished" or bad things can be expected.

The "underfeeding" test was made on two pens of rats. One pen full was fed in the regular way, and the rats died in 650 days.

The other pen was fed on a diet considered deficient in certain elements which doctors say one must have or suffer serious consequences.

This diet was considered deficient in calories. The rats did not grow so fast, but they lived 1105 days —or 70% longer than the rats fed in the regular way.

The test showed that rapid growth portends rapid decay and early death. This is true of both plants and animals. Yet parents want their children to grow fast and be fat.

Over-eating produces various disorders, rapid growth, and short life.

What constitutes over-eating? The amount of food eaten by those who have access to all they can eat and made, more-tasty, by the cook to promote gluttony.

Three big meals per day is over-eating; yet that is eating according to the doctor's orders.

Most people eat not only three times per day, but much between meals. At regular mealtime they may not be hungry but eat for fear something bad may happen if they don't.

Doctors declare that it is inviting danger to miss a meal. That failing appetite shows something is brewing in the body, and the appetite should be intensified with a tonic.

We seem to have found one phase of the Law of Longevity that ruled in the days of the biblical patriarchs.

They did not develop fast, they did not mature fast, they did not age fast, and they did not die fast.

Adam was 130 when he begat his first child and lived 930 years *(Genesis 5:3, 5)*. Methuselah was 187 when he begat his first child and he lived 969 years *(Genesis 5:25, 27)*.

We pass on to Arphaxad, grandson of Noah, who begat his first child at the age of 35 and lived only 438 years (Genesis 11:12, 13). Peleg, great grandson of Arphaxad, begat his first child at 30 and died at 239 *(Genesis 11:18, 19)*. Nahor, eight generations after Noah, begat his first child at the age of 29, and lived only 148 years. *(Genesis 11:24, 25)*.

As men grew faster, they matured faster, grew old faster, and died faster.

It appears that before the Flood it required a century for man to reach maturity, and he lived nearly 1000 years. Doctor John Gardner, of England, in his book on Longevity, writes:

"Before the Flood men are said to have lived 500 and even 900 years. As a physiologist, I can assert positively that there is no fact reached by science to contradict or render this as improbable. It is more difficult, on scientific grounds, to explain why man dies at all, than it is to believe in the duration of human life over a thousand years." (page 267).

There are no orthodox physicians and surgeons and few naturologists who possess sufficient knowledge of the body's physiological processes to understand the secret of the body's rejuvenative powers.

Fasting is unnecessary when feasting is absent and a man is in good health. He who eats only what the body requires has no need to fast. But that man is seldom found. The rule is to eat in a day enough food to supply the body for several days.

Chapter No. 11
Renewal of Youth

"Thy youth is renewed like the eagle's" *(Psalms 103:5)*.

Naturologists show that civilized man's Environment and habits make his blood either the Sparkling River of Life or the Stagnant Stream of Death.

As the toxins of the cells accumulate in the blood, due to man's filthy environment and faulty habits, the body becomes flooded, choked, and poisoned by its own excrement.

Despite the fact that man follows a faulty course of living and dwells in a hostile environment filled with polluted air, the constant renewal of his body tissues holds decrepitude at bay for a considerable period of time; and some men, even under these adverse conditions, manage to live for a century or more.

Natural scientists show that fasting rejuvenates the body because it frees the vital channels of clogging waste and allows the renewal process to balance that of disintegration; that it permits the body to purge itself and clean house, normalize its fluids, correct its chemistry, and come closer to a state of equilibrium.

Professor Morgulis, in his famous work on fasting, related specific instances of Rejuvenescence. He said:

"The acuity of the senses" is improved by fasting, and "at the end of his 31 days" abstinence from food, Professor

Levanzin could see twice as far as he could before the fast began."

Carrel asserts that "life lengthens if animals are fasted during certain fixed periods," and that "man's longevity could probably be augmented by analogous procedures" (page 180). He adds, "Fasting purifies, profoundly modifies and improves our tissues" (page 229).

Naturologists show that nerve force, during a fast, is conserved and transmitted in more powerful waves to the vital organs, enabling them to improve in function and to eliminate more fully the toxins which accumulate in the blood under steady feeding.

In some cases, "the degree of re-juvenescence will not be so great in a decrepit man of 65 or 70 as in that of a man of 45 or 50."

Doctors Carlson and Lunde, University of Chicago, showed that a fast of fifteen days temporarily restores the tissues of a man of 40 to the physiological condition (age) of those of a youth of 17.

Astounding! Rejuvenescence is a fact. But medical art is not interested. It lives and thrives on human misery and not on human health.

Not only does fasting halt the onward march of physiological age for man as it does for worms, but it even turns back the hands of measuring time for him as it does for worms. Why not? All animals are subject to the same Cosmic Law.

The Ancient Masters often spoke of cases of rejuvenation, but their accounts have not been understood by a world in darkness. Now we can read their writings with more understanding —

"His flesh shall be fresh as a child's; he shall return to the days of his youth. And thy youth shall be renewed like the eagle's. These things worketh God oftentimes in man" when man knows how to live in harmony with the law *(Job 33:25, 29; Psalms 103:5)*.

According to the findings of Carlson and Kunde, a man of 40, under the beneficial effect of fasting, regains 23 physiological years of life. That means a man of 63 solar years would be only 40 in physiological years of life.

An account in the press of February 27, 1938, stated that Tapsi Dishan Das Udasi, of India, was reported to be 178 years old but "appeared to be not over 40." He claimed to know the secret of rejuvenation, but would tell no one.

Physiologists hold that as the cells of a man of 40 can be regenerated to equal those of a youth of 17, it is impossible to keep them indefinitely in that condition. For it is easier to hold that which man has than to regain that which he has lost. If that is possible, then it is certainly within the limits of that possibility.

By exhaustive experiments, Morgulis showed beyond the shadow of a doubt that fasting is a dependable and certain process of regeneration. He found that during a fast the body does not tear down its tissues nor impair them structurally.

The tissues are merely reduced in size as in the case of the worms. They decrease in bulk but not in number.

Another secret of the process of regeneration is that the nuclei of the cells lose so little bulk under a fast that they become relatively larger in ratio than the rest of the cell, as in the case of children. Such cells have the same capacity for development that characterizes the cells of children. This is further evidence that fasting rejuvenates.

After the fast has purged the blood of toxins and the body of clogging filth, healthier cells replace the degenerate cells.

That is the amazing work of the Process of Regeneration. But fasting results cannot be accomplished in the case of those who refuse to improve their habits and fail to move to a better environment.

Experiments have consistently shown that the less one eats the longer one tends to live and that as the food intake is gradually diminished, the intra-organic adaptive functions of the organism adjust the glands to the new condition. If this course is continued, the time will come when a large meal, such as the man was formerly accustomed to eating, will be such a burden on the digestive system as to cause much discomfort, if not a case of illness.

During World War 1, the Carnegie Institute conducted a series of experiments that proved much in this respect. A group of healthy young men, some of whom were athletes, were kept for months on a diet of very spare proportions that reduced the men to ten percent below the weight they had maintained on their regular diet, although none of them were fat.

By the lean diet the men developed into about the same physical condition as the spare, wiry, rawboned men of the type that live longest. Yet on the meager diet there was no evidence of any loss of physical power.

Many studies and measurements were made which did not show any marked physical changes, with one exception, and that was favorable. In every case there was a marked decrease in pulse-rate, accompanied by lower blood pressure. These are good signs.

The test showed that the most certain and striking effect of a spare diet is that of decreasing the labor of the vital organs, of the heart and circulatory system, of the stomach and bowels, of the liver and kidneys — of all organs of elimination that break down so early in life from excessive work.

These experiments show that elimination is more important than feeding. On the excreting part of the body processes, the maintenance of the vital condition is more intimately and immediately dependent upon elimination than upon the supply of new aliment,

Feeding may be suspended for a considerable period without causing more than transient debility. But the steady removal of the effete particles produced by the constant disintegration of body tissues cannot be checked for even a minute, in warm-blooded animals, without inducing fatal results.

For every act of respiration is in effect one of excretion, of elimination; and to stay the breath is to quench the life. One case is sufficient to show what is possible in millions of other cases, as Cosmic Law never changes nor varies.

At the age of 30 one Bertha Fried, 5 feet 1 inch tall, Temple Garden Apartments, Baltimore, Maryland, weighted 196 pounds. Like others, she subsisted on the regular orthodox diet, recommended by the physicians and surgeons.

She decided to give Nature a chance to reduce her weight and took a series of fasts, gradually increasing the duration and fasted forty days in thirteen weeks. Her weight dropped to 134 pounds, and her form, previously coated with ugly fat, now presented a firm, shapely appearance.

She has since fasted forty days each year. This year (1951) was the only exception, when circumstances prevented; and she fasted only eight days, taking nothing, not even water, and lost only two pounds. During these eight days she conducted physical culture classes with the same zeal and energy as ever, and all who saw her were amazed.

Born October 9, 1901, she is now in her 56th year and feels, acts, and looks like a young woman in her 20s. Doctors who have examined her are amazed at her excellent condition.

In 1942 she studied under Joseph Pilates, 939 8th Avenue, New York City, who teaches Contrology — a good form of exercise, consisting of posture, breathing, and various body movements. She is a qualified physical culture instructress. Cycling and walking are her favorite exercises, but she enjoys any form of activity, including running. She can walk twenty miles a day without difficulty at the rate of 4 m.p.h.

Eating is no economic problem for her now. She eats but once a day — in the evening. Her food consists chiefly of fruits. She eats little so-called protein foods and never feels hungry.

When she first changed to one meal a day seventeen years ago, there was a slight desire for the other meals due to habit, but that soon vanished.

She appreciates the value of outside air and sleeps outdoors when weather permits, regardless of how cold it may be. The floor is usually her bed. She retires early and rises early. She sleeps soundly and can go to sleep at will. Her conscience is clear, uncluttered with fear, worry, or discord.

She uses cornmeal instead of soap in bathing. Soap cuts the natural oil from the skin and makes it harsh. To give tone and glow to her clear skin, she uses a brush and finds it invigorating.

(Note: The skin of man is delicate and should not be irritated to produce vigorous reactions. That is the primary effect. The secondary effect is lasting and will be disappointing, as the skin will show the sad result of the harsh treatment. — Hilton Hotema)

Her stamina is exceptional, her personality radiant, her manner friendly and magnetic. She is calm and at ease with the world, yet full of energy and enthusiasm. She is a student of yogi, practices the postures and exercises, and enjoys the breathing exercises in fresh, pure air. She likes the sunshine and has a nice sun-tan.

As is usual in such cases, she has gone on to develop her mental and astral properties. While meditating she receives much benefit and experiences a calmness that envelops her whole being.

Chapter No. 12
Man Once Lived 80,000 Years

"There is no natural death. All deaths from so-called natural causes are merely the end-product of a progressive acid saturation." — Crile.

"All creatures automatically poison themselves. Not Time but those toxic products produce the senile changes we call old age." — Empringham.

"The cell is immortal. It is merely the fluid in which it floats that degenerates. Renew this fluid at the proper intervals and give the cell proper nourishment and, so far as we know, the pulsation of life may go on forever." — Carrel.

"There is absolutely no reason why man should die." — Thomas A. Edison, inventor.

"There is no physiological reason known at the present day why man should die." — Doctor William A. Hammond, late Surgeon General U. S. Army.

"Death is not a primitive attribute of living matter; it is of secondary origin. There are animals that never die." — Professor Weissmann.

"In the years to comes when man learns more about how to live, he will never know illness and will live for thousands of years." — Professor I. S. Haldane.

"The human frame as a machine is perfect. It contains within itself no marks by which we can possibly predict its decay. It is apparently intended to go on forever." — Doctor Monroe.

"With a perfectly balanced endocrine system, such as a normal man has, one should live forever. In fact, your Fountain of Youth lies within yourself." — Doctor Friedenburg, N.Y.

"At his creation, man was endowed with the power of Perpetual Youth." — Sir Isaac Newton.

"A continuous change goes on in the substance of the entire body by which its materials are constantly dissolved and constantly renewed. Throughout the whole system, vital force is incessantly engaged in disintegrating the tissues of which the body is composed and in building them over again of new and fresh materials, so that all the tissues of the body are always renewed and always ready to perform their allotted work." — J. C. Dalton, M.D., Professor of Physiology, New York College of Physicians & Surgeons.

Dalton describes above the process of Perpetual Youth. Due to the work of this process, man's body is completely renewed in from one to seven years. Seven years is the longest estimate of physiologists. This means that regardless of the number of years, man lives, his body is never more than seven years old.

This fact was referred to by Professor A. E. Crew, Edinburgh University, in addressing a Social Hygiene School at Cambridge, Massachusetts, when he said:

"It is of the utmost importance that we should once and for all free ourselves of the notion that death is a necessary attribute or an inevitable consequence of life. It has been abundantly demonstrated that Life can and does continue without ceasing.

"Given appropriate and necessary conditions of environment, Eternal Youth is in fact a reality for living forms. It is possible to take a worm and by repeated processes of fasting, keep it alive twenty times longer than it had lived in the regular way. There is no physiological reason known why similar treatment of man should not bring about similar rejuvenation.

"There are no mysteries of Life and Death, only ignorance. As knowledge increases, so will man's power over his physical environment and over the mechanism that is himself. Science as well as religion affirms that in the future mankind may, if it be so desired, not only remain permanently youthful, but also may live forever."

In 1904 Harry Gaze wrote a book titled *"How to Live Forever,"* in which he said:

"The fact that the body is in a process of continual change has not been sufficiently recognized. Until the discovery of the principles of physical immortality, no effort was made to adjust the Mind to this change.

"In order permanently to renew the body, the Mind must be in harmony with the change; but this humanity has hitherto failed to do. In position contradiction to the Law of Renewal, man had steadfastly believed the body to be gradually growing older until it is no longer able to perform its function."

Man steadfastly believes what medical art teaches — that the body does wear out and grow old. When medical health officers die in their 50s and 60s, it is proof that medical schools are in darkness concerning the Law of Physiology.

Carrel writes, "Man is composed of soft, alterable matter, susceptible to disintegration in a few hours. However, he lasts longer than if he were made of steel. The body seems to mold itself on events. Instead of wearing out, it changes. the physiological processes always incline in the direction leading to the longest survival" *(Man, The Unknown)*.

Professor Crew says that it is more difficult to explain why man dies than to show that he should live forever. Carrel actually demonstrated that man is endowed with immortality in the flesh by showing that living cells are immortal and man's body is built of these immortal cells. He cited definite reasons why man dies as follows:

"In primitive life, when men were healthy and lived longer, they were subjected to long periods of fasting. If want did not compel them to fast, they voluntarily deprived themselves of food. All religions have insisted on the necessity of fasting. It purifies and profoundly modifies and improves our tissues (page 229).

"Life lengthens if animals are subjected to fasting during certain fixed periods. Man's longevity could probably be increased by analogous or other procedures (page 180).

"Life shortens because the body cells are not completely freed of waste products by the blood. If the volume of the body fluids were much greater, and the elimination of waste products more complete, human life would last longer" *(Man, The Unknown)*.

The faults Carrel cites rise not from defects in the body's construction and constitution and advanced physiologists show that they may be corrected and prevented by living within the Law of Life.

It is recorded that the ancient Britons subsisted on acorns and berries and were still young at the age of 200 years. The modern Glutton would never think of exchanging his delicious diet for such a small reward as one hundred years of life. He says, "Why live at all if you can't have what you want?" He may have what he wants by paying the price demanded.

The press of February 1, 1930, reported that a son was born of the 57-year-old wife of a man named Mashun, living in Stalinibad, U.S. of S. Russia. He was 116 years old; and the woman was his 17th wife.

The press of July 11, 1922, reported the death of John Shell of Greasy Creek, Kentucky, U.S.A., at the age of 134. His wife was 122 when she died.

Zora Agha, a Turk who visited the U.S.A. in 1930, died in 1933 at the age of 160.

According to the records of Saint Loenhard's Church, London, Thomas Cam died in 1795 at the age of 207.

Li Chung-yun of China died in 1933 at the age of 256. Numes De Cugna of India died in 1566 at the age of 370. Dando, the Illyrian, lived over 500 years. These cases appear in recorded history; and what these men did is possible for millions of others to do.

"What is there to age a man in the turning of the earth on its axis," asked Waite.

Decrepitude, called old age, is a condition of the body that is not the work of years; and somatic death is not the work of Time but the end of a course of degeneration.

Linn E. Gale wrote: "Science agrees that death can be deferred and Life extended far beyond the prevailing limit. Some scientists go far beyond that and assert that disease and old age will eventually be eradicated to such extent that death will be the exception instead of an unfailing rule, as at present." — *Health Messenger,* June, 1928.

In Volume II of his work, *"Life and Teachings of the Masters of the Far East,"* Baird T. Spalding said:

"During the preceding September, we had arranged to meet a party in the Gobi Desert, and the party was to accompany us to the site of three of the ancient mined cities, the location of which is given by some of these records. While we had not as yet seen these records, we were told of their existence. Those we had previously seen had aroused our interest were but copies of the records that we had before us. Both sets of records placed the dates of these cities back over 200,000 years; and it is claimed that the inhabitants were in a high state of development, as they knew the arts and crafts and were able to work iron and gold; that gold was considered a metal so common that they used it in making drinking vessels and for shoeing their horses.

"It is claimed that these very ancient people had command of all the natural forces, as well as their own powers. In fact, the legends, if legends they are, told therein are quite similar to those of Greek Mythology.

"If the (ancient) maps are correct, this great empire covered the larger portion of Asia and extended into Europe as far as the Mediterranean Sea to about where France is now located; and the greatest elevation was about 600 feet above sea-level. It is claimed that this was a vast plain area, very productive, and well populated, and a colony of the Motherland (Lemuria).

"There is no question that, if the remains of these (ancient) cities can be found and uncovered, some valuable history will be discovered, as the description these records gave of this land far outshone that of ancient Egypt for pomp and splendor during the dynasties of its seven kings.

"The leader of the expedition turned to Bagget Irand and asked whether he would give us his version of the people that had inhabited the region and established the cities like the one that lay in ruins below where we were camping. He began by saying:

"We have written records that have been carefully kept from generation to generation for over 70,000 years. These records place the date of the founding of the city, the ruins which lie below this camp, more than 230,000 years in the past.

"The first settlers came from the west as colonists many years prior to the founding of the city. These colonists settled in the south and southwest. As the colonies gradually developed, some of the people moved north and west until they inhabited the whole land. As the fertile fields and orchards were established, they laid the foundation of cities.

"Here they built temples; not as places of worship, for they worshipped every moment of their lives. Living was always dedicated to the Great Cause of Life, and while they lived in cooperation with the Great Cause, that Life never failed them.

"During that time it was quite common to find men and women thousands of years old. In fact, they did not know (somatic) death. They passed from one accomplishment to a higher attainment of life and its reality. They accepted Life's true source, and it released to them its boundless treasures in a never-ending stream of abundance.

"But I have digressed: Let us return to the temples. These were places where written records of any attainment in knowledge of the arts, science, and history could be preserved for those who wished to avail themselves of them. The temples were not used as places of worship, but as places where the most profound scientific themes and philosophies were discussed. The act and thought of worship in those days were carried out in the daily life of the people, instead of being set aside for a particular group or at specific times." pages 71-2.

According to the press of July 30, 1948, Doctor W. C. Psi, research fellow of the Chinese National Geological Survey who unearthed "the Peking Man's remains in 1929," says "We know that there was a dawning of human life in China fifty million years ago — the Peking Man proves that."

Recent excavations in the Gobi Desert reveal remains of cities of a prehistoric civilization approximately two hundred thousand years old.

In 1948 U. S. Army fliers in this region found a gigantic pyramid, reported to dwarf the Great Pyramid of Egypt. It was estimated to be 1500 feet wide by 1000 feet high, with a base covering approximately fifty acres. Its great age cannot even be conjectured.

The above statement of Bagget Irend undoubtedly refers to the Breatharian Age, when man lived in harmony with "The Great Cause," and life never failed them. They lived on and on and "did not know (physical) death."

Doctor Kenyon Klamonti shows in his work titled *Man's Unused Powers* that in his physical perfection man did not eat nor drink, being entirely free of all economic burdens and receiving all substance required by his body from and through his Astral Organs directly from the Air.

This information supports the ancient legend to the effect that the Ancient Masters lived so long that they knew man is endowed with the Fountain of Youth and the Power of Immortality in the flesh and could live in his physical from as long as he desired when he knew how and lived accordingly.

According to this ancient legend, some men lived 5,000 years; and "the Calmucks had a tradition that men in the first age of the earth lived 80,000 years." Certain secret Tibetan scriptures tell a similar story.

Doctor Franz Weidenreich, American Museum of Natural History, wrote in his book *"Giants and Men,"* that "man has descended from a race of giants that lived in an age far earlier than is supposed."

These mighty men of early days *(Genesis 6:4)* lived so long that they were competent to predict definite events to occur in the distant future by virtue of the accurate knowledge they accumulated thru the many centuries they lived as to the operation of Cosmic Forces, which never "progress" nor vary from their fixed and eternal course.

Some scholars assert that from this source came the men who designed and built the Great Pyramid of Egypt.

Professor Thevenin adduces evidence to show that thousands of years ago there suddenly appeared, from an unknown source, in the land now known as Egypt, scientists and philosophers with a knowledge of astronomy, geometry, physics, chemistry, mathematics, and mechanics so extraordinary, who had scientific instruments of such precision, who knew the secrets of the Universe so well, and who employed their own knowledge so skillfully that their work, contained in and displayed by the Great Pyramid of Gizeh, is still miraculous and beyond our comprehension.

Modern man's life span is so short that he has not time to learn much, while his mind is rigidly controlled for fear that he may learn too much.

When an ambitious man happens to get too far ahead of the social pattern, he is silenced and disposed of by the "powers that be." For established institutions depend for existence upon the rigid preservation of that social pattern which gave them birth.

Hesiod, living about a century after Homer, stated that there was a time when men enjoyed Perpetual Youth, sinking into a death-sleep without pain when he was ready to return to his original home in the Great Invisible World.

Another ancient scribe declared that early man were healthy, and their days were long; that returning years saw them still in their prime, and the length of their life was so great that counting their days wearied even the wings of Measuring Time.

The biblical scribe wrote: "For as the days of a tree are the days of my people." — *Isaiah 65:22*.

Man in the early days was never sick. Illness was unknown, doctors there were none, and somatic death was a voluntary act. Man simply sank into a deep, deep sleep, voluntarily induced by his own will power and left the physical world and returned to his permanent home in the Astral World, leaving us the knowledge that somatic death may be deferred as long as desired and that when death comes, it is only a change which brings the end of the physical form, but not of man *(1 Corinthians 15:51, 52)*.

The press of January 27, 1935, reported the discovery of the fact that a big lizard called the Iguana, found by Doctor Paul Bartach of the U. S. National Museum, in a little-known island of the West Indies, can produce its own demise anytime it desires. Some will "commit suicide" when captured.

These Ancient Teachers said, "Though the outward man perish the inward man is permanent. For our light affliction (somatic death), which is but tor a moment, worketh for us a far more exceeding and eternal weight of glory" *(2 Corinthians 4:16, 17).*

Drugless Methods

With the increase in drugless methods and a corresponding decrease in medical methods, health improves and life lengthens.

The press of May 16, 1954, stated, "The United States today has 4500 citizens over 100 years old and older, bolstering the belief that man is the longest lived mammal on earth."

In what part of the USA did these centenarians live? The report showed that too. It said, "All northern states, but one, listed no one in that (centenarian) category." ... All the southern states claimed large numbers, ranging to 40 in Mississippi, 41 in Alabama, and 51 in Texas.

Those who have studied the matter assert that the surprising increase in the number of centenarians is due to the combined work of all the various health agencies and influences, which show that medical art is actually a system of shortening life by destroying the body with its many poisons.

Osteopathy was announced in 1874 by Doctor Andrew T. Still, its founder, a skilled surgeon of the medical profession. At an early period in his professional career he lost several of his own children that had the best care that medical art could give.

That heart-breaking experience convinced him that the "practice of medicine is basically wrong," and caused him to search for a better method. This was the driving force that founded the school of Osteopathy in 1892.

Then came Doctor D. D. Palmer and Chiropractic. He made his first adjustment of a vertebrae in 1895.

Nothing more seems to have been done until 1903, when his son, Doctor B. Palmer, established a school to teach Chiropractic.

Two years later, Doctor Willard Carver, a lawyer who had taken care of the legal end of Doctor D. D. Palmer's work, founded the Carver Chiropractic College at Oklahoma City, Oklahoma.

Chiropractic teaches that "to section the Spinal Cord induces degeneration; pressure on the Spinal Cord induces paralysis; constriction on a special spinal nerve causes disorder in all tissues beneath. Section, pressure, and constriction are related terms, each producing its degree of effect.

"The steam-fitter closes a valve to cut off the steam; the plumber shuts a faucet to stop the flow of water; the electrician pushes a button to stop the flow of electricity.

"The same process applies to man. Any section, pressure, or constriction reduces the flow of vital force from brain to tissue cell, where function is expressed."

But section, pressure, and constriction are not necessary to reduce the flow of vital force from brain thru spinal cord and the nerves out over the body. Reduced flow may result from weakened brain, deteriorated spinal cord, and defective nerves.

The drunkard staggers and may fall because liquor has affected his brain, spinal cord, and nerves.

A sober man may have the same symptoms by breathing polluted air. Men who work in garages, truck drivers, and motorists are often half-drunk due to the inhaling the poisonous exhaust fumes, to the soft drinks they take, and to the drugs and serums of medical art.

All substances used by medical art are poisonous to the body, a fact admitted by medical doctors. They would not think of giving to the well the poisonous substances they give to the sick, knowing it would be dangerous and yet believing that the sick body can take what the well body can't.

In addition to osteopathy and chiropractic, other systems have been born because medical art is such a gross failure. We have naturopathy, orthopathy, hygienists, naturists, etc., all of which are proving successful where medical art fails.

This fact is shocking and frightening to medical art, and it works harder and harder for more laws for protection as it sees itself slipping and for ways and means to crush its worthy competitors.

You cannot leave the USA for a foreign land without being vaccinated and inoculated. You cannot send children to school, in free America, unless they are vaccinated and inoculated. You cannot serve in the armed forces without being vaccinated and inoculated. You cannot even go to prison without being vaccinated and inoculated.

This wholesale system of blood-poisoning is having a serious effect on the people.

And all of this medical control in spite of the fact that millions of people in this country do not believe in the theories of medical art and condemn vaccination and inoculation.

It is interesting to observe that the centenarians live in the southern part of the USA, largely in the hills and outlying regions that are rather free of medical control.

Salt Eating Dangerous

When did any doctor ever tell a patient that salt eating is dangerous? In Colliers of November 26, 1954, T. D. Ratcliff wrote: "Body fluids — a Major Medical Problem."

Under that headline he said: "This year some 200,000 Americans will drown — not in oceans nor pools, but in their own body fluids. The cause is often congestive heart failure, as big a killer as cancer."

He says that congestive heart failure is often the cause of excess fluids in the body because —

"When diseased hearts are unable to pump enough blood to the kidneys, those organs fail to excrete the body's surplus fluid; and it congests tissues, feet, legs, and ankles swell with retained water, a gallon or more may accumulate in the abdomen or chest."

This statement leads the layman to believe that blood from the heart goes directly to the kidneys as it does to the lungs. Such is not the case.

All blood from the heart, except that which goes to the lungs, leaves the left ventricle of the heart thru the great aorta, main trunk of the body's blood system. Then thru its many branches the blood is distributed to the entire body, the kidneys receiving their supply thru branches from the aorta termed renal arteries.

To increase the blood flow to the kidneys requires an increase in the general blood flow thru the aorta to all parts of the body, as occurs in vigorous exercise.

Ratcliff believes in the exploded medical theory that the heart is a pump. It is a valve, not a pump. It is the great central valve of the blood vascular system, regulating the blood flow, not pumping blood.

Then he lets the cat out of the bag. The accumulation of excess water in the body is not due to "diseased hearts." It is due to salt eating.

He says: "An ounce of salt in the body will seize and hold three quarts of water."

If salt eating is responsible for excess fluids in the body, if salt eating is the reason why "this year some 200,000 Americans will drown win their own body fluids," what is the remedy? Stop eating salt.

Ratcliff is careful to see that the doctors are needed. He does admit that "low salt diet helps" but says:

"In the fight against water death, doctors today rely on kidney-stimulating drugs. A new drug of this type, Diamox, is already being ranked as a major medical discovery."

There it is — pure medical propaganda. The purpose of the story is just to promote this "major medical discovery."

Why not correct the condition by not eating salt? That would leave no place for doctors and Diamox.

Back to Nature

In his *"Back to Nature"* magazine in 1936, Doctor St. Louis Estes, frequently called the "Raw Food King" said so much against salt — "Salt — The Death Dealer," that his article was reprinted in the May 1937 issue of "How to Live" magazine.

In the article was quoted a letter from a wise naturopath, giving his observations of salt eating. He had a patient suffering from Bright's Disease; and upon examination, he found there was a small excretion of salt.

As so little salt was being eliminated, it occurred to him that the salt was accumulating in the body, and water accumulated to lessen the irritation of the salt.

It was not the case of salt seizing and holding the water, as stated by Ratcliff. It was the body's demand for water to lessen the irritating effects of the salt. It was the tissues of the body holding the salt.

The patient was in the dropsical condition so typical of this disorder in advances stages so he placed the patient on a salt-free diet. In three days the dropsy disappeared.

To be sure of his ground, he tried this three times with the same result. Each time the patient was given salt, the dropsy returned; and each time the salt was withheld, the dropsy disappeared.

Doctor G. J. Drew, another "raw food king" of the 1939s, wrote:

"Salt is so stable that it is not dissolved and utilized by the body. It is ingested as salt and excreted as salt.

"As the salt is absorbed by the body cells, they contract from the irritation and discharge their precious albumen and other vital elements. This causes hardened arteries, tissues, shriveled blood corpuscles, arthritis, and produces the state called old age." *(Unfired Foods.)*

Hal Beiler, M.D., said: "In the days of our forefathers, salt solution was used as an embalming fluid. The ancient Egyptians used salt oils and spices in their mummy wrappings.

"Today we mummify the living with salad dressings made of salt, oils and spices, and see them walking the streets. Their dry skin, shrunken bodies, and enervation bespeak of hardened blood vessels, livers, kidneys, and muscles.

"I often wonder why it is necessary to embalm such bodies after death. They are already pickled to the gills." *(Philosophy of Health)*

Most primitive people in their natural state use no salt. Bartholomew found Chinese of the interior ate no salt. Doctor Benjamin Rush found the American Indians never ate salt when discovered by the white man.

Stomach ulcers and some cases of blindness are due to salt. Glaucoma is one of the most prevalent and serious of eye ailments, causing about one in eight cases of blindness.

In the normal eye a thick fluid flows into and out of the eye at a constant rate. In glaucoma, exit channels for the fluid become blocked by a waterlogged state of the body. Internal pressures rise. Vision becomes distorted; a rainbow halo appears around lights. If not relieved, the pressure continues to rise, eventually producing much pain. In time the optic nerve terminals are destroyed and blindness follows, due to salt eating.

Mr. A, age 39, paralyzed from the waist down, limbs emaciated, was given up to die by the best doctors. He used salt freely. It was impossible to move the muscles of his limbs. A wise naturopath had all salt removed from his foods, and at the end of four days he could move the muscles of his toes.

Mrs. B, age 50, was unconscious for three days from uremic poisoning, was told by three physicians that she would die of Bright's Disease. A wise naturopath had all salt removed from her food, and she recovered health.

Thousands of cases could be cited where the sick recovered health by simply living on a salt-free diet.

Sodium chloride (salt) conceals itself in the cells and tissues like a thief in the night, and irritation begins that calls for water.

This eventually produces hypertension of the nerves, deterioration and hardening of blood capillaries, blood vessels, high-blood pressure, all forms of growths, including cancer and tumor, arthritis, psoriasis, neuritis, valvular leakage of heart, defective hearing and eyesight, and is in fact the root of many ailments.

Ratcliff's 200,000 a year who drown in their own body fluids can thank their salt-eating habit for that.

The basic cause of not congestive heart failure, as claimed by Ratcliff. It is the result of salt eating.

Frederick Hoelzel, after years of experimentation, declared that the cause of mental and physical deficient cases is due mainly to a "retention of salt and water in the body."

He relates in his book, *Devotion to Nutrition,* that his experiments showed that salt eating, with the retention in the body of salt and water, impairs the body's functions.

Many people suffer from "hidden edema," due to salt. The most common symptom of this condition is a swelling of the ankles. Hoelzel showed that the cause is salt eating. He also showed that "salt retention, hypersensitivity of the skin, thickened skin folds, and fat deposits are interrelated."

The Breath of Life

Scientists agree that city air is a deadly mixture of smoke, soot, and fumes, which include carbon monoxide gas, sulphuric acid gas, benzene, methane, sulphur-compounds, and other dangerous chemicals too numerous to mention.

In addition, city air is saturated with the fumes of motor cars, trucks, buses, gas engines, etc. This exhaust gas consists of carbon monoxide, carbon dioxide, lead oxide, lead carbonates, free gasoline, and complicated benzene chain compounds of the hydrocarbon series.

Let us consider just one of these many poisonous gases, carbon monoxide, and tell only a small part of the damage it does to the body.

Tasteless, colorless, odorless, invisible to the eye, this gas takes and has taken a terrible toll of lives in our cities in the last 30 years.

The large cities have a huge smoke blanket over them that holds down the gases, especially in damp weather, and tends to smother the people.

U. S. Authorities have demonstrated a concentration of 0.62 parts of carbon monoxide per 10,000 cubic centimeters of air at street level in busy sections of cities of 500,000 populations or more.

There are few poisons that are more deadly than carbon monoxide. Air containing as little as 120th of one percent will cause headache, and 150th of one percent will cause total collapse.

Doctor L. Burns examined blood specimens of more than 20,000 persons to discover the effect of carbon-monoxide gas on the body. He said: "Carbon-monoxide gas seeps into the blood thru the lungs and mixes with the hemoglobin to such an extent that the blood cannot perform its normal function of carrying oxygen to the rest of the body."

The hemoglobin has an affinity for this gas about 300 times greater than for oxygen, making the absorption of the gas by the blood very rapid.

The first symptoms of this poisoning are headache and weakness. More serious symptoms appear as the condition progresses. People are told in food propaganda to eat this and that kind of food to offset this weakness.

Scientists of Harvard, risking their lives to discover more about the effect of poisoning by carbon-monoxide gas, found that the average man can endure it only until his blood is one-third saturated.

The danger of the gas was shown by the way it affected one of the scientists. He had just completed some tests requiring a high degree of skill and was feeling no ill effects of the gas when he suddenly collapsed and had to be carried out and revived.

Small concentrations of the gas can soon bring a man to the breaking point. Five percent of the cars and trucks on the roads have sufficient concentrations of the gas to be a menace to drivers and passengers.

There is no natural nor acquired immunity to the gas. Repeated exposures produce the same effect each time.

Many who drop dead or die suddenly are not afflicted with heart disorders as doctors claim. The cause of death is polluted air.

The annual report of the Bernard Free Skin and Cancer Hospital asserts that city dwellers, breathing polluted air, "develop lung cancer" at a rate three times greater than inhabitants of rural districts.

The Mellon Institute of Pittsburgh issued a report of a two-year survey covering the damaging effect of polluted air on human health. The report said:

"The inhalation of polluted air results in a gradual absorption by the body of the poisonous products. The insensible intake results in a condition of slow-poisoning, which insidiously eats away at the vital tissues."

The Chicago Health Department reported that in certain sections of that city the sulphuric acid gas in the air rots clothes hung on wash lines and eats away building stone and metal guttering.

These acids and gases in the air corrode and destroy in time everything within reach. They eat up stone and steel; they eat up clothing and metal guttering; they eat up the body cell by cell. Many of the symptoms of the eating process appear as mysterious "diseases unknown to medical science."

The corrosive acids in the air attack cells and tissues, throat, nose, lungs, brain. They attack the heart, liver, spleen, kidneys, and sex organs.

They attack the blood corpuscles and cripple them so seriously that they cannot carry on their normal function. That condition medical art terms "anemia."

They attack the nerves, and the resulting pains medical art calls "neuritis." As the nerves weaken, paralysis may result.

They attack the cells of the muscles, producing dull pains that puzzle medical art, and medical doctors cover up by terming it "rheumatism."

They attack the tissues of the joints, and medical art calls it "arthritis."

They attack the tissues of the air cavities of the cranial bones, and medical art calls it "sinusitis."

They attack the throat, and medical art calls it "laryngitis," "tonsilitis," "diphtheria," etc. Hoarseness often follows, and in time one's voice weakens or may be entirely lost.

They attack the cells of the blood vessels of the heart, and medical art calls it "heart disease."

They attack the cells of the lungs, and medical art calls it "tuberculosis."

They attack the cells of the pancreas, and medical art calls it "diabetes."

Names, names, names that mean nothing aside from indicating that part of the body wherein degeneration is most serious and active from the actions of poisons in the air. Medical art, rules largely by superstition and speculation, and being nothing more than a modernized version of ancient voodooism, makes a confusing mystery of what it calls disease for profit and greed. The problem is readily solved by the recognition of a few simple, basic principles.

Polluted Air of Southern California

The air of Los Angeles area is exceptionally bad. The Los Angeles Herald said: "Heavy clouds of smoke cling close to the ground intermingled with smarting fumes that make people bleary-eyed and gasp for breath."

The account stated that "bleary-eyed men" were watching factory chimneys to discover the source of damaging fumes that killed small animals in adjacent residential areas. During the worst of the "gas attack" nine out of ten persons on the streets were "bleary-eyed" from the smarting fumes.

This black pall of smoke makes a ceiling over Los Angeles from 1500 to 2000 feet high.

John F. Gernhardt, M.D., of Los Angeles, stated that more than 30 persons in the city died of heart attack in 24 hours.

Polluted air was the cause. It paralyzes the breathing centers of the brain and breathing stops. It paralyzes and that is not heart attack.

The press reported that southern California has lost about 60 percent of its valuable sunlight due to the smoke pall hanging over that area.

Flowing Air

Still air, like still water, grows stale, stagnant, and poisonous. Doctors appear not to know that.

Windstorms, tornados. and hurricanes are cosmic processes of air purification. Another secret of Nature and yet not discovered by medical art.

But the discovery was made by a layman who did some thinking. He wrote a book published in 1944, titled *Floating Air.* (By Joseph Conbole.) It is hard to get a copy now, as medical art feared the valuable health information it contained and high-pressured the post office department to put it out of circulation.

This man first tested his theory on poultry and was able to relieve in a few hours, bad cases of croup and kindred respiratory ailments.

That was bad news for medical art; and it must be suppressed, for there is no money making possibilities on air.

In his chicken house, this man put an electric fan to keep the air in motion, thus dissipating the foul fumes of poultry droppings, the inhalation of which makes chickens sick. How many poultry raisers know that?

Very simple. Too simple; a deep secret of Nature the doctors have not discovered.

Doctors go the other way. They favor still air, being careful to warn people to avoid drafts of fresh air. They favor the bad and condemn the good.

This man knew the same law that applies to chickens also applies to man. So he put an electric fan and ventilators in his bedroom, drawing in fresh out-side air and driving out the stale inside air.

Most homes and bedrooms are filled with stale air, unfit to breathe. People follow the advice of doctors and keep windows closed to keep out those "deadly drafts" of fresh outside air.

Even the gases and vapors expelled by the body are poisonous and pollute the home and bedroom, regardless of whether from lungs, bowel, or the pores of the skin.

When these facts are known, it is easy to understand why people get up in the morning with cold, sore throat, and other respiratory disorders.

They blame the weather; so do the doctors. But it does not affect that way the animals that live out in it. The actual cause of it is the polluted air in home and bedroom.

So remarkable were the good results this man obtained that he was inspired to build up his "Miracle cabinet," consisting of a bed with enclosed sides and top, well ventilated and introducing air-conditioning electrically with a fan thru special vents.

He used the cabinet first for patients with respiratory ailments, such as colds, hay fever, sore throat, diphtheria, asthma, influenza, pneumonia, and tuberculosis.

The good results were amazing, and he was encouraged to treat in the same manner patients with all kinds of disorders, fever, mumps, measles, rheumatism, neuritis, diabetes, etc.

His remarkable success proved that good, fresh air in motion will "cure" the sick who have failed to respond to long medical treatment. He got patients well after medical doctors had cast them off as incurable physical wrecks.

No Diseases

He proved what a few great doctors have declared: that there is no disease. There are just two conditions of the body — Good Health and Bad Health.

The symptoms of Bad Health the doctors are trained to study, group together, and give them names (diagnosis) that mean nothing and term them diseases that are trying to kill the patient.

That scheme is supported by centuries of false teaching, by which medical art has created a false psychology of disease, that yields gigantic profits. Medical art is one of the biggest frauds on earth.

The surprising results of this man's work with air shocked medical art. Drugs, vaccines, and serums were becoming obsolete. Something had to be done.

It was better one "man should die for the people," that medical art, perish not. *(John 11:50).*

So the heat was turned on the post office department, and this "man died for the people." This man's great work of helping the sick, after medical doctors had failed, came to a sudden and inglorious end.

In such cases big publications carry lying propaganda, that a certain quack who was a menace to the people has been cast into oblivion. And the people believe.

Medical propaganda leads people to believe that medical art is trying to rid the world of so-called disease. Who can be so silly as to think that any organization or institution is working to bring about its own end?

The reason why people do believe it is because "better schools" make "better communities." That is another one of the lies taught in the schools and people just grow up in it from childhood.

The facts show that all methods orthodox medical schools do not teach, regardless of their value and effectiveness, are banned and crushed by medical art, and these unorthodox practitioners are usually put in prison — all for the "protection of the public health."

This may not be in Russia, but many Russian methods are used to dispose of those who interfere with the money-making schemes of big business.

Body Construction A Mystery

Medical art declares and believes that man eats to nourish his body. Like most medical theories, this one begins to shake when closely examined.

All authorities agree that the body, its organs and parts, all come from the parent cell. That Cell is not the product of food, and what food does not produce it cannot sustain.

All authorities agree that body growth results from cell division and subdivision. Then what part does food play in the process?

Recent discoveries in the realm of atoms have exploded many medical theories, and more such explosions are coming.

Medical art admits that the body is composed of Cells. The Cells are not composed of food nor produced by food.

Body cells are composed of atoms; and an atom is a constellation of electrons, a colossal reservoir of force, none of which comes from food.

Milliken, a truly great scientist, in his book, *Science of the New Civilization,* said, "Electrons are the building blocks of the Universe," and the earth, vegetation, and all animal bodies are composed of these "spiritual blocks."

An atom is a miniature solar system with "planets" (electrons) circulating within the infinitesimal system of the atom, around a common center of attraction, at a speed of from 10,000 to 90,000 miles a second.

It would require 340,000 barrels of powder to give a bullet the speed with which some electrons dart in and out of their groups.

A gram of hydrogen (a tiny portion of the simplest gas) contains enough power to lift a million tons more than a hundred yards.

On the lowest computation, there are in the cortex of man's brain at least 600 million billion of these arsenals of power. And medical art stupidly claims that man's energy comes from food.

The chemical atom is so small that it requires a billion to make a group barely visible under the most powerful microscope; and a thousand such groups would have to be united to make a speck visible to the naked eye.

The microscope reveals innumerable animalcules in the hundredth part of a drop of water — a tiny microcosm filled with living beings.

To determine the composition of the body requires knowledge of the composition of the electron. Doctor H. H. Sheldon, University of New York, said:

"Electrons, long regarded as the ultimate substance of which all matter is formed, have been known to have a reality only as a wave form, while an atom consists of a bundle of such waves."

"We as individuals have no existence in reality other than as waves, multitudinous and complicated centers in the ether. . . . We are analogous, in a sense, to the sound that issues from a piano when a chord is struck."

Electrons are condensed centers of whirling force in the ether.

Carrel held that the body is not built of extraneous material, He said: "An organ . . . is not made of extraneous (external) material, like a house ... It is born from a cell and the house originated from one brick, a magic brick that would begin manufacturing other bricks from itself . . .

"An organ develops by means such as those attributed to fairies in the tales told to children ... It is engendered by cells which, to all appearances, have a knowledge of the future edifice and synthesize from substances (apparently) contained in the blood plasma the building material and even the workers" (*Man, The Unknown,* pages 107-8).

Carrel contradicts himself. He said the body is born from a cell that begins making other cells by a process of division and subdivision. Then these additional cells do not come from substances contained in the blood plasma, but from the original Parent Cell, as stated.

To a cosmic ray scientist, we put this question: Is it possible to nourish the atom? He said, "Yes; they are constantly being nourished, accelerated by their nucleus."

Of what does the nourishment consist? His answer: "It is the 'Air of Life' that nourishes the nucleus of all atoms of all organs in the body. This Air, at all times present and perpetual, is the Creative Substance of All Matter!"

This takes us back to Anaximenes (380-320 B.C.) who said: "The Essence of the Universe is in the Infinite Air in eternal movement which contains ALL in itself" *(Man's Unused Powers,* book 3, page 28).

The nourishment of the atom consists not of crude physical food, but the Air of Life. Then why does man eat? What part does food play in the body?

Hotema answers this question by stating:

"Cell and body nutrition is a myth. What man consumes as food does not supply nutrition by assimilation as science teaches. The ingested substance produces activity in cell function by stimulation, not by nutrition."

"Two types of stimulation seem essential for the function of living cells; vital and chemical. The vital comes from the Air of Life, while liquid and food supply the chemical."

"Ingested substances contact and stimulate the cells into certain activity and leave the body thru the eliminative channels, as flowing water turns the wheel of a mill, activating the machinery that does the grinding and passes on without every becoming a part of the mill or its machinery" *(Nutritional Myth,* page 17).

Carrel exposed the ignorance of science as to living things when he said:

"Those who investigate the phenomena of Life are as if lost in an inextricable jungle, in the midst of a magic forest, whose countless trees unceasingly change their place and their shape. These investigators are crushed by a mass of facts which they can describe but are incapable of defining in algebraic equations" *(Man, The Unknown).*

Professor Wilfred Bransfield in an article titled *"Continuous Creation,"* said that the substance of living things comes from the Air. As to the trees, he wrote:

"In tree life, so much comes from the air and so little from the soil ... Every change, every new intro-atomic spatial re-arrangement of protons, neutrons, and whirling electrons, every addition or displacement of electrons, sets up vibratory resonance ... building up atoms of higher mass. The reactions are electrical, and it is useless and foolish to apply chemical methods."

And still modern biologists believe that the "secret of Life" will be found in new physical and chemical discoveries.

Doctor Philip S. Haley, Director of the California Society for Psychical Research, reported in his work *"Modern Loaves and Fishes"* some interesting cases of those who live without eating, such as the one of Angelina Van der Flies who fasted for 35 years.

The press of January 3, 1954, reported that Doctor Paul M. Laughton and Doctor D. C. Mortimer, two members of the Canadian National Research Council, showed by test that the leaves of sugar beets changed air into solid wood in 10 seconds.

The leaves were exposed to small amounts of carbon dioxide gas under a bright light. The gas was first made radioactive so it could be identified when it got inside the plant. The leaves were allowed to absorb the gas for varying periods and then were killed in boiling water.

Radioactive cellulose was found in the leaves even though they had absorbed the gas only ten seconds.

The body's laboratory changes the Air of Life into blood, bone and flesh, and the food one eats produces activity in cell function by stimulation, not by nutrition.

Mystery of Man

According to the Bible, God formed man of the dust of the ground and breathed into his nostrils the breath of life and man became a living soul *(Genesis 2:7)*.

That is another theory of man that was fabricated by the Bible writers out of their own imagination. They never copied that statement from ancient writings. It is erroneous in its entirety. The Ancient Masters knew the constitution of man too well to make that silly and absurd statement.

We shall show by logical statements that man's body was not and is not formed "of the dust of the ground" and that "the breath of life" does not make him "a living soul."

In our work titled *The Mysterious Sphinx,* which all should read, (available at www.frontlinebookpublishing.com), we showed that the four different animals composing the Sphinx represent the constitution of man. That was the secret reason why the Sphinx was constructed.

The Sphinx, The Four Fixed Signs of the Zodiac, and the Great Pyramid of Gizah symbolize the Four Cosmic Principles which constitute man.

The Bible describes man as having three bodies, viz., (1) Soma Pneumatikon (Spiritual Body); (2) Soma Psychikon (psychic body); and (3) Soma Sarx (Physical Body).

The Ancient Masters did not divide the psychic body as we do. They considered it a unit, whereas we divide it into two sections, the subconscious or subjective, and the conscious or objective.

We showed in our work titled *Kingdom of Heaven* (available at www.frontlinebookpublishing.com) that the word "consciousness" is unique. It is a coined English word. Its equivalent appears in no other language, and it was not used by the Masters. The word is formed by the union of two Latin words, con, with; and scio, to know; and literally means "that which we know."

The Zodiac is a chart that represents the Temple of Man during his earthy peregrinations. It symbolizes the Four Cosmic Principles which constitute man, as follows:

1. Solar Radiation, the Spark of Life, or Solar Body.
2. Air, the Breath of Life, or Psychic Body.
3. Water, the River of Life, or Mental Body.
4. Dust of Earth, the Body of Life, or Physical Body.

The Zodiac determines the color of the astral vibrations, the note or number of man, and how he will use his divinity while in the flesh.

Man corresponds in color, number, and vibrations to the solar system at the moment of his birth. He is clad in the zodiac.

According to the Masters, Mind is present in Matter and is conditioned by Matter until Mind rises superior to Matter and controls it — as in the case of the ancient wise men, sages, and seers. That high state will never be attained by the masses who suffer from a rigid state of Mind Control.

The Zodiac teaches how Solar Man becomes embodied in a prison of matter and how the Mind is inseparable from the cosmic elements.

The Spark of Life, the Solar Body, has been given various names, such as True Being, Logos, Nous, etc., and it is said that the Nous is the archetype, the Archeus, the Primal Element of substantive objectivity, that which becomes by differentiation, first the subtile, and then the gross material elements of the manifested worlds.

Like most definitions touching the vital principles of Being, this one just takes us back another step and leaves us there in the dark.

What is "the vital principle which presides over the growth and continuation of living beings?"

That vital principle the Ancient Masters revealed in their writings, but their writings were destroyed by the church to keep the masses in darkness.

The vital principle we have listed in our work on the Sphinx, along with the other Cosmic principles which constitute man.

From the Archetypal World (that of the Logos) there emanates successively the Psychic and the Material bodies of man.

The Psychic Body presents two distinct departments, consisting of the subjective (Subconscious Mind) and the Objective (Conscious Mind).

It is correct to term the Subjective Department as the Psychic Body and the Objective Department as the Mental Body. Neither is that a case of splitting hairs, as the Subjective functions when man is unconscious; and the Objective or Mental Body is blank and functionless.

Solar Man is the hero of the Apocalyptic Drama. He appears as "the Conqueror" when one of the seals was opened, as stated in *Revelation 6:2,* and his number is 1,000.

Revelation treats of the Serpentine Fire as we have stated in our work titled *The Magic Wand* (available at www.frontlinebookpublishing.com), and its energizing thru the Seven Seals of the Book (vital nerve centers of the body), by the means of which the conqueror gains mastery over the Five Senses, symbolized by the Five Kings which Joshua captured and subdued *(Joshua 10:5, 10).*

Then the Conqueror builds up for himself, out of the primordial substance, his immortal vehicle, the monogenetic or Solar Body.

He is that deathless body (Soma Heliakon) and is symbolized in Revelation as a city that descends from the sky, enveloped in the radiance of the Sun *(Revelation 21:1, 2).*

Man's body is a materialization of the invisible gases of the air, consisting of electrized and intelligized atoms, making the body the visible manifestation of the Solar Pattern of the Archetypal World. Truth is such a rare quality, a stranger so seldom met in this world of fraud, that it is never received freely, but must always fight its way into a controlled social order.

Chapter No. 13
Self-Denial

If any man will come after men, let him deny himself and follow me *(Matthew 16:24)*. That may sound good, but we don't see many devout Christians putting the precept into practice.

Man controls his destiny and works out his own salvation. The primary step in his improvement is that of rigid self-denial. He that overcome the (all desires of the flesh) shall inherit all things (good in life); and I (Perfection) will be his guide, and he shall follow me in health and happiness *(Revelation 21:7)*.

Poverty, want, and sickness are the work of man. They are the legitimate products of his evil habits which correspond with his desires. He increases his burdens as he increases his wants.

The less man needs the more complete he becomes. He gains in his struggle for Perfection as he gains freedom from his Wants. The more Wants he has, the less complete he is, and the farther he inclines from Perfection. Man changes his world when he changes himself.

Man's improvement is opposed by every institution on earth, by every business organization, by every medical system, by every money-making scheme and even by modern theology.

On January 12, 1951, Frank W. Abrams, Chairman of the Board, Standard Oil Co. of New Jersey, made an address before the National Citizens Commission for Public Schools; and his address was so highly considered that it was publicized and widely circulated. Among other things, he said:

"There can be no doubt that we are discussing something very fundamental to business when we talk about education. ... If only to maintain and expand its markets, the business world has at least as big a stake as anyone in the achievement of an educated, productive, and tolerant society. ... There is a definite correlation between education and the consumption of commodities. Education has done more to create markets for business than any other force in America."

That is the orthodox view and, according to that view, the purpose of education is to maintain and expand the markets of business, and to credit demands for commodities. To that end billions of dollars are expended annually in the education of the children of the U.S.A. And to that end a catchy slogan has been invented to the effect that "Better Schools Build Better Communities."

The constant cry of Commercialism is to consume more, create new markets and new demands, promote the production of commodities, employ more wage slaves, increase the economic burden. The art of living in harmony with the law, a secret known to every bug, bird, and beast, is so lightly regarded by civilization that it receives no attention. He who gets so far ahead of the multitude as to oppose

Commercialism and the Social pattern, is promptly silenced, disgraced, and liquidated for the "public good"; and the press carries huge headlines proclaiming that another enemy of social progress has been jailed. The deceived multitude listens and believes.

One's teaching may be in perfect harmony with the Cosmic Plan of Life, the Law of Perfection, and the Science of Cosmic Economy; but that brand of teaching does not harmonize with civilization's artificial world, nor support its system of Commercialism, nor its social pattern, therefore it cannot be accepted, tolerated, and supported by any institution or any form of government. It must be suppressed "for the good of the people."

Tell us how long man's artificial wants and unnatural desires will mean money for Commercialism, and we will tell you how long man will remain in his present condition of degeneracy and economic slavery.

Under the ruling and conflicting conditions of civilization, man has little chance for self-improvement.

The wealth of the world is pitted against him. So he has no place to look for help. He must depend on his own efforts, powers, and resources. He must make himself a social outcast if he would rise above the social pattern and thus bring down upon his head the infamy, ridicules, opprobrium, sarcasm, and hatred of the world.

So very true is the statement put in the mouth of the gospel Jesus that the world hated him "because I testify of it, that the works thereof are evil" *(John 7:7)*.

And with the centuries they grow worse instead of better.

As we ponder these facts, we see more clearly why the Ancient Masters were persecuted and murdered, why their valuable works and writings were destroyed, and why they wisely recorded their discoveries of the Mysteries of Life in puzzling parables and perplexing symbols. He who is ready to face the fury of the mob, the ridicule of the rulers, the persecution of the powerful, let him take up the burden of enlightening the masses and march forth into the dreary waste of "no man's land." Then he will understand why the Masters of Modern times remain in dark seclusion.

Economic Freedom

It is both interesting and important to note that as man moves back toward the great simplicity of Primal Perfection, his wants decline and his economic burdens decrease.

We thus learn what these burdens are and whence they came. We see them as the product of man's created wants and unnatural desires which Perfect Man had not. Man has produced them, and he alone can destroy them.

It was not until man began to form bad habits and adopt artificial practices which created his wants that he began to decline and degenerate. He was deceived then, as he is now, by the illusion of progress as he developed new habits and increased his wants. He believed then, as he does now, that each new invention was a mark of progress that led him to a better life, while he and the doctors were puzzled by the fact that his health continued to decline and his life span to decrease.

Economic Freedom is the first step back toward man's high estate of Primal Perfection.

Every bug, bird and beast, in its native state, has economic freedom. Man the master of the earth is the only economic slave upon the earth. He has made himself that by his artificial wants and acquired desires.

In complete freedom from every want, to be dependent upon nothing, man's mind and senses are under control. He is released from the consequences of action, which are bonds and chains, binding down those who are the slaves of want and desire.

Ancient Secret of Personal Power: Tetragrammation

Good Health is the very foundation of Success. And we have heard health is man's birthright. That is another grievous error. Good health is the reward received by him who earns it. Contents: *Kingdom within, Perfection is within, Secrets of the Body, Mysterious Glands, Seven Astral Centers, Tetragrammation, Science of Sensology, Edocrinology, Higher Consciousness, Theology, Seership, Astral Light, Living Fire, Macrocosm, Time-Eternity.*

Ancient Sun God

Contents: *The Ancient Light, The Great Sun God, Secret of the Stars, Astrology Changed to Astronomy, Virgin Mother, Majesty of God's Kingdom, The Sovereign Sun, Ab-Ram the Sun-God, Lamb of God, Perfection.*

Awaken the World Within

Contents: The Course of Study, 58 wonderful lessons. *These lessons show how the higher faculties of mind and soul may be aroused and activated, thus enabling the body, through which the real man contacts the physical plane, to express the noblest characteristics. If you are seeking the highest spheres of mental, physical existence, you should find in these lessons the help and guidance you need.*

Cosmic Science of the Ancient Masters

Contents: *If a man die, shall he live again? Is reincarnation a fact? The sublime truths of the Universe. The Mysteries of Nature, of Man; The Grand Cycle of Creation, Conscious & Subconscious Mind, Intuition, Immorality, Dormant Organs, The Mysterious Chambers in the Skull.* Highly Illustrated with rare Occult Illustrations.

The Kingdom of Heaven

Contents: *The Grand Cosmic Kingdom and its Seven Parts. The Mental Kingdom; Consciousness and Super-consciousness; Why People Fail; Freedom and Slavery; The Spiritual Organs and Powers; The State of Brahma; Telepathy and Television; The Fourth Dimension.*

Living Fire or God's Law of Life

Contents: *The Ageless Wisdom of the Ancient masters tells us that the Divine Trinity is reflected in man, and his Knowledge, when correctly and clearly interpreted as Hotema has presented it in his various works, will lift the veil that darkens the Mind and reveal to the understanding of man the facts of Eternal Life.*

The Magic Wand

Contents: *The Serpentine Fire, its energizing through the subtle body centers (chakras): Mastery over the senses; Awakening of the 6th and 7th senses; The Black and White Serpent; The Golden Oil of Kanda; Biblical truths that have been Suppressed.*

The Magic World

Hotema tells a private story about himself that he has never before told in his writings. Contents: *Magic Intelligence, Magic World, Magic Esotericism, Magic and Mystery, Magic Creation, Magic Message, Magic Spirit, Magic Kingdom, Magic Wires, Magic Sensology, Magic Chambers, The Magician, Magic Light, Magic Attraction, Magic Mate, Magic Practice, Magic End.*

Man's Higher Consciousness

Contents: *The author claims this work shows the reason why the radio and television mechanism in the human skull fails to respond fully now to cosmic radiation as it did twenty thousand years ago, when the Ancient Masters accumulated their wisdom of Creation, Life and Man, then recorded it in fable and fiction, for interpretation to those who proved by test they were worthy to receive the same. The author covers subjects such as daily exercise, vegetarian diet, raw foods, sunbathing, periodical fasting, deep breathing, history of longevity, cosmic forces, secrets of the ancient masters.*

The Mysterious Sphinx

Contents: *Why is it an object of awe and reverence. A startling expose showing how a symbol for the ancient masters evolved into the God of Christianity. The secret of the Cosmic Principles which Constitute Man; The Lost Word; The Vital Principle of Life; How the Masters Communed with the Cosmic Powers and Principle; How symbolism Develops Man.*

The Magic Temple (Forthcoming Spring 2019)

Contents: *The amazing powers of the human body. The author says the world is still trying to solve the mystery of man. Is God as described in the first book of the bible? The evolutionists refuse to consider that fabulous account, and assert that man is the product of creation. People grow up in that confusion and know not what to believe. There is no death, as religion teaches. Food does not build blood as science teaches. Food doesn't give nourishment to the body as taught by the dietitians. Man need not die at 100 years. He quotes scores of unusual facts seldom found in the average textbook.*

The Mystery of Man

Contents: *The cosmic process of transforming solarized man into physical man, Illusions, The dual aspect, The identity of ego, The secret of the atom, Doctrine of numbers.*

The Facts of Nutrition

Contents: *The variety of the organism depends not on the food and drink, for experience teaches athletes to go into action with empty stomachs. The author gives his concepts that the growth of the body does not result from food consumption, but from the division and subdivision of the parent cell. What food does not and cannot produce, it cannot and does not sustain.*

The Genesis of Christianity

Contents: *Hilton Hotema started in Sunday School — he went regularly until he was fifteen. At twelve, he began the study of the Bible in earnest. He became a preacher and after preaching in scores of different states and finally found the truth was not being given to the people. He began comparing the various Bible and religious books and found many startling facts which were never given to the people from the pulpit ... never taught in public schools, nor in Sunday Schools. He found the average preacher knew a little about the history of the bible, and was shouting about things that were not true. He discovered why the Roman Empire was plunged into mental darkness with the birth of Christianity. That darkness was necessary to help the priesthood frighten people, to keep the priesthood in high places, and to drive the multitude into the church, for the sake of profit and power. He shows why Moses could not have written the Pentateuch (The first five books of the Bible — the account of his own demise — Deuteronomy 3)*

The Glorious Resurrection (Forthcoming Spring 2019)

Contents: *Symbolism; Ancient Science; Crucified Saviors; Great Mother of the Gods; Mysterious Resurrection; Birth of Gods; Light; Two Bodies in One; Ancient Terminology; Mystic Sleep; Life Swindle of Mytheography; Unknown Joy of Death; The Future Life; Reincarnation; The Universal Fable.*

The Golden Dawn

Contents: *Those who mourn the dead will be most interested in this work. The Golden Dawn, sharply gleaming on the distant horizon, denotes the approach of a brighter day in the life of man, the Lord of the whole world earth (Zechariah 4:14). The millions of innocent people, sustained by fear of death, sees the brilliant signs and shudders. For the sign heralds the revival of knowledge that will inform man of the mysteries of creation and liberate his mind from fear of death. Man will learn that he is life, and that life has no beginning and has no ending. What appears as death pertains only to the body and not to life. The body was never alive. It was only the mechanism used by life to perform certain work of creation in the visible world.*

The Great Law

Contents: *Professor Hotema studied the teachings of the Ancients from hidden and revealed sources for over seventy years. He was a student of many movements and teachings, Rosicrucian, Theosophy, Hindu, Hebrew, Egyptian and Grecian Mysteries, Magian Tradition, Masonry, the Tarot, Arcane Sciences, Hygiene, Vegetarian, and many others of which the world has never heard. He delved into ancient records and gathered scattered and widely separated fragments of truth from the ruins of temples of the Masters who were so far ahead of us in knowledge and wisdom that only the few can interpret their true meaning. And he has interpreted it, boiled it down, condensed it into readily comprehensible material.*

The Great Red Dragon

Contents: *Ancient Scriptures, Tree of Life, Thou Shalt Surely Die, Act of Propagation, Coition and Convulsions, Pituitary Tumors, Sin Unto Death, Card 6 Temptation, Woman Appears first, the Degenerate Woman, Man a Degenerate woman, analysis of Homosexuality.*

The Secret of Regeneration (Book I)

Contents: Some of the 128 Chapters — *Truth, The Dark Ages, Age of Ignorance, Age of the Earth, Age of Man, Sunken Continents, The Antediluvian World, Ancient Cultures, People of Atlantis, Despots and Tyrants, Nineveh and Assyria, The Chaldeans, The Hebrews, Israelites in Egypt, Driven out of Egypt, The Babylonian Captivity, The Scriptures of the Jews, The First Forgery, The Priest and the Scribe, The Second Forgery, The Pentateuch, The Third Forgery, Story of the Exodus, Biblical Contradictions, The Fourth Forgery, The Synoptic Gospels, Many Gospels, The Work of the Priesthood, The Need for Gospels, The Essenes, Pious Fraud, Ecclesiastical Lying and Forgery, Argument Against Christianity, Is Jesus a Myth/ Deceiving the Masses, How the Church Triumphed, etc., etc., etc.*

The Secret of Regeneration (Book II)

Contents: Some of the 84 Chapters — *Sex Symbols, The Garden of Eden, The Tree of Knowledge, The Serpent, The Sons of God, The Law of Nature, Evolution vs. Devolution, Law of Cause and Effect, The Perfect Man, Degeneration of the Gods, Sex and Seed, Similitude of the Sexes, Rudimentary Organs, Appearance of Woman, Law of Variation, The Hermaphrodite, Amativeness, Sexual Consciousness, Asexuality, Auto-Sexuality, Degradation of Women, Sex in Religion, Morality & the Church, Woman under Church Rule, Traces of Woman Rule, Marriage, Woman the Superior, Is Coition Natural for Men, Coition & Convulsions, The Virgin Mother, Preventing Impregnation Mentally, Fornication & Imagination, Woman Appears First, The Degenerate Woman, Man a Degenerate Woman, Perfect Man Born, Not Made.*

The Divine Life

Contents: *What is Life, Dust of the Ground, Breath of Life, Law of Creation, Law of Change, Creative Force, Origin of Life, Kinds of Life, Hidden Artist, Man is Not Life, When Man Begins to Live, Relation of Man to Life, Man Does Nothing of Himself, Influence of Tradition, Ancient Worship Rules Today, In Spirit and in Truth, What is the Soul? The Mysterious Force, What is Intuition, Voice of the Soul, Divine Intelligence, Why Men are Mocked, Death Penalty of Disobedience, The Great Commandment, How Long Should Man Live? Fountain of Youth, Human Intellect, Was Man Born to Die, Influence of Suggestion, Conditions of Eternal Life, How old is the Body, From Master to Slave, Where is Hell? Where is Heaven? Doctrine of Atonement,*

Return to Obedience, Life Eternal, Dust Returns to the Ground, Spirit Returns to the Creator, Life Eternal, World of the Dead.

Live Longer

Contents: *Right Living, Healthful Environment, Climate, Man's Home, The Artificial World, The Art of Living, He Lived 370 Years, Law of Change, Fountain of Youth, Man Once Lived 80,000 Years, Self-Denial.*

Empyreal Sea: How High Do You Climb: Live 1,400 Years

Contents: *The Human Temple, Man Created Perfect, The Aging Process, Secret of Living, The River of Life, The River of Death, Breathing, Eating, Food the Killer, Living Without Eating, Law of Adaption, What is the Empyreal Sea? Search for Longevity, The Perfect Organization, Man's Place in Creation, The Creative Power, The Divine Curse, Marriage, The New Age, Procreation and Expiration, Degeneration.*

For Orders or More Information Visit/Contact:

Frontlinebookpublishing.com
or
info@frontlinebookpublishing.com

More Praise For Professor Hilton Hotema

"Your writings have entirely changed my course of thought and so enriched my life that I am eager to read everything you have written and in my consciousness there is a deep sense of gratitude toward you."

— E. Los <u>Angeles, California.</u>
—

"I have been reading books on Health and Philosophy for more than 40 years. "May I say that the books written by Professor Hilton Hotema, which I recently purchased from you, are by far the most instructive and the most original I have ever read. I am at a loss for words to give adequate praise to Professor Hotema. Assuring you of my great satisfaction and wishing your company a well-deserved success.

— I remain, <u>L. G. T. Coronado, California."</u>

"I want to express my complete satisfaction for Professor Hilton Hotema's writings, as I find his books very stimulating and educational for sound thinking. Please add the additional books I have selected".

— <u>Thomas Mazucci,</u> New York.

"My wife and I have completed your Hotema Folio (12 books), for the second time. If I could be granted one wish for the greater good for the human race it would be, that every man and woman should read this folio at least once. We have been members of the Rosicrucian Order for many years, and the lessons and instructions covered many of the things in the folio, and prepared our minds for a better understanding."

— George O. Keefer, Los Alamos, New Mexico.

"I have just finished reading *"Man's Higher Consciousness,"* by Professor Hilton Hotema. I think it is a most wonderful book. I think it is the whole truth. I wish I had the information it contains earlier in my life. Many thanks to Professor Hilton Hotema.

— Edmund Groben, Indiana.

"These books have forced me to revise, somewhat reluctantly, of course, a good many of my former 'College degree' ideas about the whole subject of Health. This I am glad to do because now, for the first time I have a clear picture framed in my mind of both the 'beginning and the end' — as it were of what it means to attempt true healing in patients. I would insistently recommend these books to everyone interested in knowing the true facts, especially those whose mission it is to help an ailing Humanity".

— Doctor Amil H. Sprehn, Member International Society of Naturopathic Physicians.

www.ingramcontent.com/pod-product-compliance
Lightning Source LLC
Chambersburg PA
CBHW060858280326
41934CB00007B/1097